BACK TO CAPE HORN

Rosie Darling
Children of Cape Horn
Libras Don't Say No

BACK TO CAPE HORN

Rosie Swale

COLLINS
8 Grafton Street, London W1
1986

William Collins Sons & Co Ltd
London . Glasgow . Sydney . Auckland
Toronto . Johannesburg

BRITISH LIBRARY CATALOGUING IN PUBLICATION DATA

Swale, Rosie
Back to Cape Horn.
1. Chile——Description and travel——1981–
I. Title
918.3′04647   F3064

ISBN 0–00–217415–4

First published 1986
Copyright © 1986 by Rosie Swale

Photoset in Linotron Imprint by
Wyvern Typesetting Ltd, Bristol
Printed and Bound in Great Britain by
T. J. Press (Padstow) Ltd, Padstow, Cornwall

For Chile,
a country now part of me,
and for her proud and
generous people

ILLUSTRATIONS

ACKNOWLEDGEMENTS

I should like to express my gratitude to the many people who had faith in me and who helped me in very different ways to spin the threads of what was just a dream into a practical adventure.

They include, in England, Jeffrey Simmons, my agent, who had faith in my idea; Roger Schlesinger of Collins who had the courage to commission my book; Lorenzo Prieto, Cultural Attaché at the Chilean Embassy in London; John Pilkington and Hilary Bradt, authors of *Backpacking in Chile and Argentina* (and especially John, who read my manuscript and saved me from a multitude of errors); John Brooks, editor of *The South American Handbook*; Major Bill Beldham of the RAVC for his advice and the loan of an invaluable packsaddle and other equipment; Dai Bowen, veterinary surgeon, for much advice; John and Jane Majors; and Treorchy Male Voice Choir; Bill Addison; Stanley Solomons; Glyn and Joyce; Govan Davies; Lynette Davey and Bobbie Butlin of Viasa; Nigel and Shane Winser of the Royal Geographical Society Advisory Service; and, after my journey was over, Dan Franklin, my editor at Collins.

The following firms kindly provided equipment for the journey: Ultimate Equipment Ltd (Phazor Dome tent and Mountain King sleeping-bag); Damart International Ltd (thermal underwear, gloves and balaclava helmets); Karrimor International Ltd (rucksacks); Powerhealth Ltd (Ginseng capsules and other assistance); Helly Hansen Ltd (thermal jacket); Spall Leisurewear Ltd (tracksuits); Space-coats Ltd (thermal coat); Laboratoires RoC (UK) Ltd (sunbloc and face creams); Fuji Ltd (film); Rothmans (UK) Ltd (who provided life and medical insurance); Supreme Plastics Ltd (plastic envelopes and containers); Hiram Walker International Ltd (for a case of Ballantine's whisky on my homecoming). I must also thank Pembrokeshire Health Authority for medical advice and free vaccinations.

In Chile I must thank Germán Claro Lira and his family, of Hacienda Los Lingues, for the loan of Aculeo Hornero and Aculeo Jolgorio; Carlos Jelvez Martínez, Regional Director of Tourism in Antofagasta, for unstinting assistance and advice; the people of Antofagasta; Bob Hand and his family for photography and much other help; General Mendoza Duran, and all his carabineros, who showed such kindness to me and the horses; Margarita Ducci, National Director of Tourism, and her assistant Mónica Krassa; René and Marcella Varas; Professor Bente Bittman; John Hickman, British Ambassador in Santiago, and his wife Jenny; Matthew Hickman for his assistance with photography; Veronica, Germán Claro Lira's secretary; Dr Antonio Ayuy, Hornero's and Jolgorio's vet since foalhood; Jean Laing de Walbaum and the great G. K.; the children of Esquela Chimbaronga; Hugo Donoso Pavéz; Rodeo Club Florida; Pinto Rodeo Club; the jumping stables in Chiguayante; Erwin Neito Gómez, who nursed Jolgorio in Chiguayante, and his wife Sara, who nursed me. I would also like to say a special thank you to all the vets and horse nurses who helped us on the journey; also to Bayer Ltd for their offer of veterinary supplies.

Thanks are also due to the vagabonds on the beach in Chaitén, who made Hornero a moccasin when he was lame and taught me how to make fires in the rain; Alejandro Chochair Lemús ('El Aysenino Porfiado'), for his help and for teaching me something about social conditions in Chile and how to fish; Nora 'Mi Casa' Chaitén; Maurice

10

Mannakee, who sent medicines for Hornero; the cavalry squadron at Villa Santa Lucía, especially Official de Ejército Marcelo Hernández and horse nurse Luis Parada; Juan Andrade and his family for the sheepskin chaps; Roberto Vieras Frías, comandante of LSM *Elicura*, and his crew; Margot Duvalde and her housekeeper Margarita Cayupi, who spoilt me; Carlos Soto, Governor of Punta Arenas; Armando Miranda Paredos and his family in Puerto Natales; Nora Castro and her family; Bill Matheson, Honorary British Consul in Punta Arenas; Gonzalo Campus Lira of the ferry *Río Cisnes*; Germán Fuenzalida Leyton of the Lancero Cavalry Squadron in Puerto Natales; the owner and captain of the ferry *Ro Ro Evangelistas*; General Mattai and General Fernando Rojas Vender for flying me to Teniente Marsh Base in Antarctica, and the women of the base for their kindness; Admiral Merino, Admiral Pheifer and Admiral Camús of the Chilean Navy for permission to land on Cape Horn; Juan Echeverría, comandante of the Beagle Channel District and Puerto Williams Naval Base. Special thanks too to the carabineros of Magallanes – even to the young man who by mistake cut Hornero's fringe.

Final tributes must go to the *Yelcho*, which took me to Cape Horn, and to her captain, Comandante García Domínguez, and his crew. And after it was all over to Coronel (R) Fernando Rojas, who with his friend Ralph Thackeray arranged to have my saddle shipped back to England.

These acknowledgements are woefully incomplete. In Chile I was shown exceptional hospitality and kindness by almost everyone I met, but it is impossible to name more than just a few of them. I can promise, however, that no one who helped or encouraged me will ever be forgotten.

ROSIE SWALE
MAY 1986

CHILE

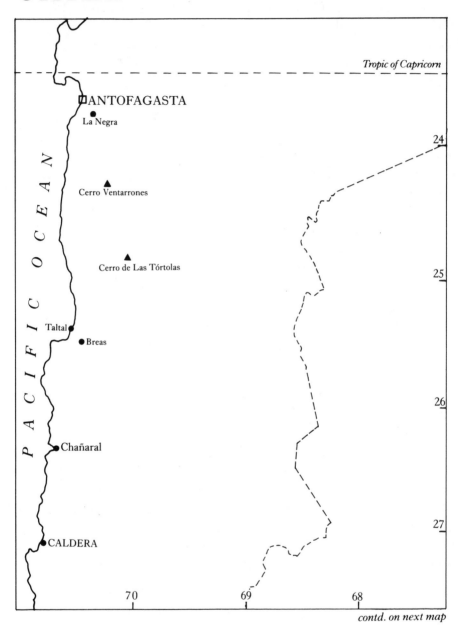

Tropic of Capricorn

ANTOFAGASTA

La Negra

PACIFIC OCEAN

Cerro Ventarrones

Cerro de Las Tórtolas

Taltal

Breas

Chañaral

CALDERA

24

25

26

27

70

69

68

contd. on next map

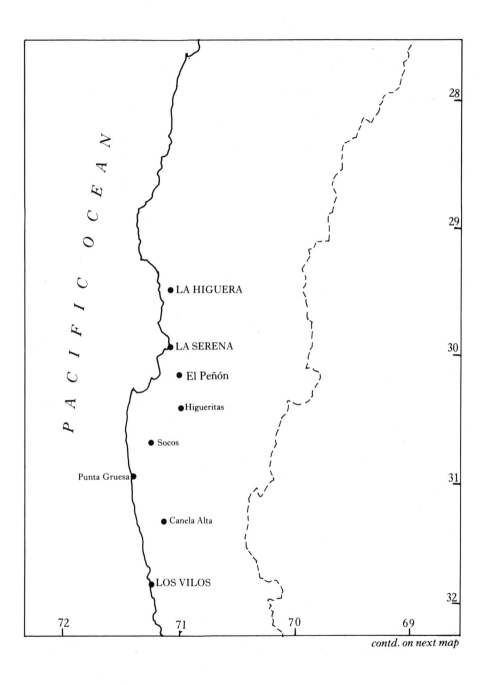

contd. on next map

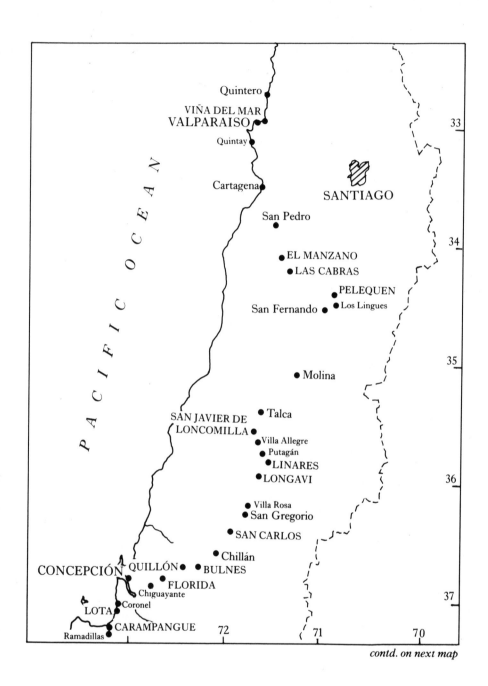

contd. on next map

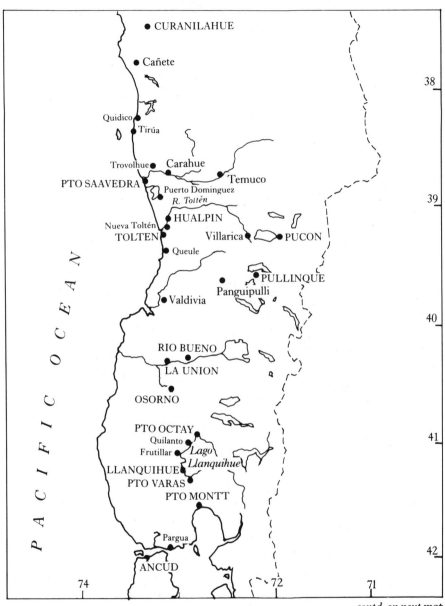

contd. on next map

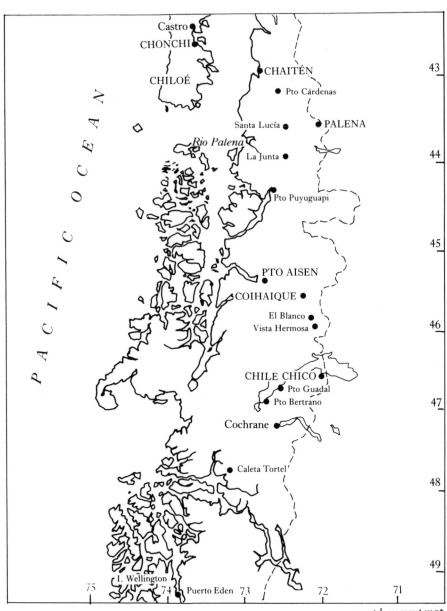

contd. on next map

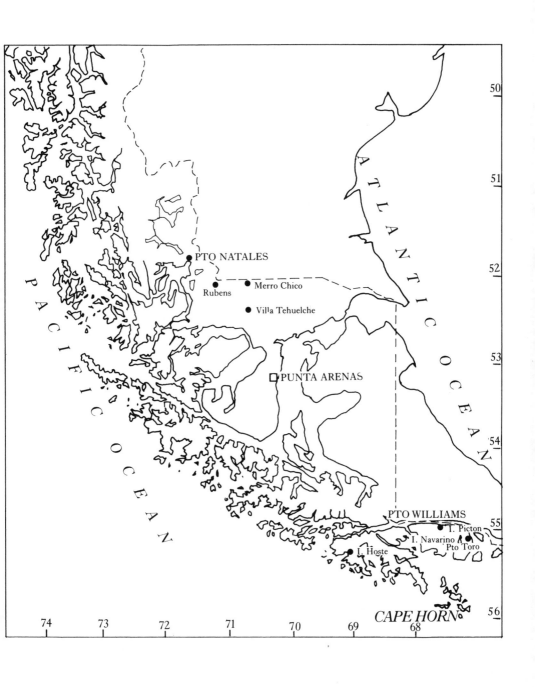

Chapter One

I believe that faith can move mountains; that genies can come out of bottles and grant wishes. Most of all I believe that if you want something badly enough, you can make it happen.

One dark evening in January 1984, while sitting in front of the fire in my cottage in Wales, I put down my glass of wine and said to myself: 'I want to go back to Cape Horn.' By the time the fire had died down that night I had the beginnings of a plan.

Eleven years before, on 8 February 1973, I had sailed around Cape Horn with my husband and two babies in a thirty-foot catamaran. It was the climax of a voyage around the world – a voyage which perhaps should never have been made. Both Colin and I were very young and perhaps we retained some of the instinct of wild animals who keep their brood with them, even through times of great danger. For eleven years images of my children playing with albatross chicks, seals, dolphins and long strings of bulbous Southern Ocean seaweed, had not left me. Cape Horn, too, had stayed in my heart. It meant more to me than any other place on earth.

I was still haunted by the beauty and magic of that day and how Cape Horn, the most dangerous sea passage of all, the grave of thousands of ships, and one of the wildest places in the world, had not betrayed our innocence.

Much had happened in the years in between. My marriage to Colin had ended, and Eve and Jimmy were now lively teenagers, at present living with him, very busy with their own dreams and education. Eve was studying for her A-levels with a view to becoming a vet. Jimmy was fanatical about karate, engineering and music.

Did I want to go back to Cape Horn to say 'thank you'? To lay a ghost? To rekindle memories? Or to find out something new?

At first all I was certain of was that my journey back to the bottom of the world should be different, special. I did not wish just to sail around Cape Horn again. Neither did I want merely to fly over it. A plan began to form in my mind. Over the next few days and nights I paced around my cottage, trying to give shape to my idea.

'The challenge this time,' I wrote in my notes, 'will be a "land voyage". I will ride alone, on horseback, from the bulge of South America down to its tattered tail and the secret landward side of the Cape, passing through the archipelago of Chile, home of only 1 per cent of that country's population, but 99 per cent of its mystery.

'I shall be riding towards the Horn at much the same pace as I once sailed past it – riding because for centuries the horse has been to adventurers ashore what the sailing boat was to those at sea, and I shall feel closer to the ghosts of those intrepid pioneers if I travel by a means which would have been available to them. Also, of course, I love horses. During my childhood in Ireland, my chief companion and confidante had been an arrogant black mare called Columbine. I had often slung bags of gingernut biscuits across her back and gone off exploring all day, imagining myself on some great adventure. The horses and I should be able to travel most of the way by land, taking ferries where the crazy jigsaw of the far south of Chile has missing pieces . . . . '

For some reason the place where I would start my adventure seemed as important as the place where it would end. My previous visit to Cape Horn was the climax of a tremendous struggle through 6000 miles of Southern Ocean. It somehow did not seem right to start my journey in Aisén or Magallanes, to return from 'just round the corner', even though I would be travelling through the archipelago, one of the most extraordinary and least explored landscapes in the world. In some strange way, the joy of going back depended on the pain of getting there.

I felt proud to live in Wales and it gave me an idea. The Welsh pioneers who had escaped the poverty of their home country at the turn of the century to face an unbroken land in South America had mostly gone to Argentina. They had settled in places like Trevelin and Esquel. In the aftermath of the Falklands war, I might not now be able to go to Argentina. Some, however, had gone to Chile, and had been among the founding fathers of the city of Antofagasta, 2500 miles north of Cape Horn, right in the middle of the Atacama Desert. 'That', I thought, 'is where I shall begin my ride.'

Not many dreams survive birth into reality. There I was, clutching my glorious idea, but very little else. I had no money to fund such an adventure and very little information as to how to go about it. My previous adventures had been seagoing ones. The sea keeps the same rules the world over. A land adventure would be different; the voyager would have to heed the laws and customs of man as well as those of nature.

Careful preparation for an expedition can make the difference between success and failure. Before I could even begin to plan my journey I had to find out the answer to one vital question: 'Can what I want to do actually be done?' 'Impossible' usually means only 'nearly impossible' and the 'nearly' is the adventure.

During the next few weeks I wrote letters and made telephone calls. My shelves bowed under the weight of dozens of books on South America. Fold after fold of the long map of Chile, a country encompassing forty degrees of latitude (seventy, if you include Antarctica), unspread on my cottage floor.

21

Señor Lorenzo Prieto, cultural attaché of the Chilean Embassy in London, John Brooks, editor of the *South American Handbook*, and John and Jane Major, who grew irregular Spanish verbs in their farmhouse in Pembroke, were just a few of those who became my professors in the mysterious new world of land exploration. I had an enormous amount to learn and they were kind, generous teachers. Eventually I was ready to confront my next problem.

Rich people can write cheques to get where they want. Poorer people have to write books, which is much harder – a fact that became increasingly apparent as I struggled for nearly a week to produce a few pages of book synopsis. I needed faith in an unborn book and an advance sufficient to finance the journey. Without this I could not begin.

'Not a good time to get backing,' everyone said. 'What happens if you spend the advance getting to Chile and setting up the adventure, then you fall down a ravine in the first week and break a leg and there *is* no book?'

'There won't be a book either if things go too smoothly and nothing unusual happens.'

'Or indeed if too many unusual things happen and you don't survive . . . '

Why couldn't I get a commercial company to put up part of the money? That's fine for something like a yacht or horse race, but the purpose of my adventure was to write a book, and how would people believe what I wrote if I had to start by saying some product was good, just because I had been paid to? I was determined that the book should be born free – unindebted to anyone except a publisher.

In a fit of optimism I had spent some of my savings on a magnificent pair of boots and started running them in over the Presili hills. They were the most expensive things I had ever worn on my feet. But the more advice I got from experts and the more I investigated the fascinating world of expeditionary equipment, the more I realized that I could not make do with a sleeping-bag, a tent, or even clothing that was unsuitable for the adventure, simply because the price was tempting. As on an ocean voyage, equipment had to be specifically chosen for quality not for cost. But what could I offer in return for some sponsorship or discounts? My only hope was to persuade a manufacturer to let me be something like a test pilot, giving an honest report afterwards on how their product had coped.

At last it was April, and quite suddenly, along with the hedgerows and daffodils of Pembrokeshire, my plans came to life. William Collins commissioned me to write the book. It is hard to describe my excitement as everything started coming together with the magic of people saying 'yes'. This is the point where a project changes into a passion, when there is no going back, because others have become as enthusiastic as you.

As soon as I received the letter of commission from Collins, I had it and my original synopsis translated into Spanish and sent them both off to Lorenzo Prieto at the Chilean Embassy. He very kindly added a long covering letter asking for all information possible, especially about the best place to buy the horses I would need for the journey, and despatched the whole lot off to his friend Señor Carlos Jelvez, Director of Tourism in Antofagasta.

Getting ready for my adventure was an education. It was also a lesson in the kindness of people. A representative from Ultimate Equipment came all the way down from the north of England and put up three tents in my large and long-suffering living-room to find out which I liked best. I chose their Phazor Dome, a free-standing 'igloo' cleverly designed to deflect high winds. Ultimate also provided me with a Mountain King sleeping-bag. Helly Hansen gave me one of their famous jackets. The Pembrokeshire Health Authority gave me, free of charge, jabs against everything from rabies to yellow fever. I was provided with vitamins, face creams, space blankets, ginseng, plastic bags and many other items.

The boots were coming along well. However I had not forgotten the other eight legs of the expedition. I haunted veterinary surgeries, particularly that of Dai Bowen, one of the most experienced vets in Pembrokeshire. He had also had considerable experience working with pack animals on the trail while in the army in the Punjab.

He showed me how to give a horse an injection; how to change its shoes; how to administer a local anaesthetic and how to sew up wounds with the bright green surgical thread he supplied me. He taught me the signs of colic and other illnesses, to watch for cuts, for bruises, for scratches, for inflammations, for damage to the horse, however slight. I had to be alert to any change in the horse, even in the expression of its eye. 'Study your horses as though you were a detective, after each day's journey,' he said.

I came out of Dai Bowen's surgery staggering under huge parcels of horse medicines. There were vitamin B12 injections to promote health and injections against almost every equine ailment. Dai's most important piece of advice, however, was about the packsaddle. 'Ask the Royal Army Veterinary Corps to lend you one,' he said. 'South American pack saddles are lethal for horses' backs.'

A week later I drove to Leicestershire, where Major Bill Beldham of the RAVC ushered me into what seemed more like a temple to tack – with saddle soap as incense – than a saddleroom. It all looked far too beautiful to touch, let alone to take on a long and muddy expedition.

Bill Beldham lent me not only a beautiful packsaddle – one of only four owned by the British Army – together with nosebags, headcollars and all sorts of other pieces of equipment, but also a handwritten manual on *Animal Transport*. It described the principles of loading up, gave instructions on the timing of stops and contained a wealth of useful information. The manual also repeated the advice I had already been given by Dai Bowen and other vets: 'The best animals to use are those indigenous to the climate.'

24

The phrase 'indigenous to the climate' stuck in my mind, much as I tried to ignore it. Although I was intending to travel through only one country, Chile has severe extremes of climate. All the experts I consulted were adamant that I would not be able to use the same two horses all the way.

This was a fundamental blow. I was not interested in simply riding through Chile, changing horses like buses as I went. My dream was to have two horses of beauty and character who would come all the way with me. They would be the protagonists of my book, and become, I hoped, my close friends and companions – much more than mere transport.

The experts emphasized that what I wanted was impossible. 'No horse', they told me, 'can within a year adapt to withstand both the heat of the Atacama Desert, and the ice of the region near Cape Horn. They will die. You must use mules or relays of horses.'

However, one man did not agree. Completely out of the blue, just three weeks before I was due to leave, a Señor Germán Claro Lira telexed William Collins offering to lend me two of his Chilean thoroughbreds. That synopsis Lorenzo had sent to the other side of the world had worked a miracle.

'My horses', he wrote in his telex, 'are from the oldest line of pure-bred Chilean horse called Aculeo, with genetic selection going back to 1760. Their ancestors were of Berber, Nubian and Arab blood and were brought over from Africa to Spain by the Muslims. Then in 1700 the most resilient of them survived the sea voyage from Spain to Chile via the Horn. Seventy-five years after this the Lippizaner horses of the Viennese Spanish Riding School were developed from the lines of Aculeo.' He went on to describe how they had been used in the War of the Pacific in the Atacama, in the Boer War and by the British in the Crimean War. Aculeon horses, it seemed, had always been sought by those who had to ask of a horse more than is really possible. I telexed my acceptance and my thanks.

On 11 July 1984 I at last left my cottage. I said goodbye to my neighbour May Evans, who kissed me on the cheek. And I said my farewells to the little church next door and to the patient gravestones, where, on sunny days, I had sometimes asked the ghosts' permission to dry my clothes.

'Those of us who live in Wales are proud to think of it as one of the last frontiers of civilization in the UK and, via its brave pioneers, who helped to found the mining industry there, one of the first in Chile,' members of the Treorchy Male Voice Choir had written, inviting me to meet them at BBC Cardiff on my way to Heathrow, and promising me a special recording of their songs to present to any Welsh people I might meet on my travels.

During my interview with these charming men an enormous box was carried into the studio. As the splendid voices singing 'Land of Hope and Glory' died down, a strange rustling could be heard on the air as – at the producer's insistence – the mystery box was unwrapped. Out came two balaclavas, two pairs of dark blue gloves, and two pairs of vests and long johns in palest blue!

In response to a frantic telephone call two days previously, telling them that these vital and firmly promised pieces of equipment had not arrived, the manufacturer, Damart, had rushed another set all the way from Yorkshire to Cardiff by Securicor van. These thermal undies were to prove much more valuable to me than diamonds, gold, or any species of freight more customarily carried by Securicor.

At Heathrow at last, standing alone amid my mountain of equipment, I kept thinking of a story my grandmother used to tell, about an Indian princess who always travelled everywhere with at least forty suitcases, one or two for her possessions, the others full of stones, just for show. It must have been before the days of air travel!

My body ached with the strain of having to lug stuff meant for eight legs. I was carrying so much luggage I could not manoeuvre myself through the door of the ladies' loo and had to suffer instead. A second crisis loomed at the check-in point. I was just wondering how I would explain that I had about fifty extra kilos in horse medicines alone and whether I would actually have to wear the packsaddle myself onto the plane, carrying bridles and headcollars as the latest in ladies' fashion accessories, when Viasa kindly came to my rescue and checked the whole lot in free. This time it was my letter of commission from Collins that had done the magic.

'What about all those jokes about sailors on horseback?' said the steward with a smile as I settled into my seat.

Chapter Two

At this time the previous year, I had been alone in the middle of the Atlantic in the tiny seventeen-foot yacht *Fiesta Girl*. There had been moments during that voyage when I believed I might never again see a tree, a blade of green grass, or another human face. Now as I flew over Paris, Madrid and Caracas to the start of my first expedition on land I wanted to keep the treasure of my sea-scoured mind, to keep my senses as hungrily and thirstily porous as they had been when I had at last arrived in New York after seventy days alone at sea.

Friday 13 July dawned to find us flying abeam of a mountain range so immense that I found it quite hard to credit that we were still on this planet. I had met the Andes. Soon we landed in Lima, a fascinating city which gave me the gift of the cheapest landfall I could make from the UK to western South America.

I had been warned that thievery is another name for poverty in Peru and as common. But nobody troubled me. One shopkeeper did rush out of his store and grab my bag. However, all he wanted to do was to tie it to my wrist with yards of twine from his shop.

Next day I flew south towards the Chilean border in a smaller plane, passing over hundreds of miles of bleak brown land. I could just make out one or two tiny settlements in cracks between endless rocks and sand dunes. 'How do the people exist?' I wondered, sipping hot coffee and eating sandwiches off my plastic aeroplane tray. 'What do they think about? Talk about?' Suddenly it occurred to me that I too would shortly be having to manage in such terrain. So – more to the point – what would *I* think about? How would *I* manage? I did not feel at all like an adventurer at this stage. I felt very vulnerable.

On Sunday 15 July I at last arrived in Antofagasta, the historic desert city just below the line of the Tropic of Capricorn, from where I planned to start my ride. I had my first doubts as to the wisdom of this as I stood outside the airport, which was some way out of town, and gazed completely stunned at my first close-up view of the Atacama. I had expected it to be desert, of course. But I had imagined this desert at least to have some scrub, some bushes, some hope! Instead, either side of the strip of tarmac for as far as I could see the terrain looked just like the surface of the moon – endless dunes of yellow pebbles and sand and in the distance great mountains.

Antofagasta city itself, in spite of its elegant office buildings and smart residential houses and hotels looking out over beautiful Antofagasta Bay, seemed, as I arrived, to be more like an island spanning the borderline between the bright blue Pacific and the solid ocean of the desert.

In spite of my worries, I was happy to have arrived. I had been thinking and dreaming of Chile for so many months that now I was here, it did not seem a foreign country at all. It was almost like coming home. Somehow I would manage, I told myself, while optimistically hoping that Fate, which had always been my friend, would not desert me now.

At least all my luggage had come through the flight safely. Or not quite all. Dai Bowen's worming paste had exploded. But the rest of the equipment had endured the many aeroplane hops more or less unscathed. 'All baggage has survived so far,' I noted in my log – including me! I left it temporarily under the long-suffering eye of a porter at one of the seafront hotels and set off down the Avenue Balmaceda.

My first stop was at the office of Mr Thursday, the local

Director of Tourism, recipient several months ago of my original book synopsis and friend of Señor Lorenzo Prieto of the Chilean Embassy in London. He had also been the magician through whom Señor Claro Lira of Hacienda Los Lingues, San Fernando, had heard about me and had offered to lend me the horses for my expedition. His real name was Carlos Jelvez. But I mixed it up with '*Jueves*' or 'Thursday' and the new name stuck.

My ally turned out to be much younger than I had expected, tall and fashionably dressed, with a friendly humorous face. He greeted me with great enthusiasm and promptly called a press conference which taxed my five words of Spanish to the limit. The Welsh music helped. When I played a little of my Treorchy song tape on one of the journalist's small recorders, several feet were soon tapping. I felt there must be a Celtic blood about. Not forgetting the promise I had made before I'd left Wales I asked about this through Mr Thursday, who spoke some English.

The reporters said that they thought there was no one of Welsh stock left in the area, though they believed that many Welsh pioneers had lost their lives in the mines when the nitrate boom was at its height around 1912. The British had also helped to build the desert railway and a British clock in Antofagasta still echoed the chimes of Big Ben.

Beneath the friendliness of the reporters I sensed some astonishment at what I was intending to do. 'Had I', it was politely asked, 'really studied the terrain?' They told me that I was now in a part of the world which had been desert ever since the land first rose above the sea, and which had never known any rain at all. Antofagasta and other ports along the empty desert coast had been built purely to export nitrates and other products from the mines. Those living there were totally dependent on lifelines of water and electricity from the mountains. Every human need had to be carried over the desert, or shipped in.

Thursday, however, remained optimistic about my project. 'Just because something is difficult,' he said cheerfully, 'does not mean that it is impossible.' His desk was strewn with maps outlining possible routes. I was astounded by all the work he had already done on my behalf. The desolate Pan American Highway, he informed me, stretched south through hundreds of kilometres of the loneliest, bleakest part of the desert. There were also some old mining tracks, perhaps shorter and more suitable for horses. However, the few settlements would each at best still be several days' riding apart. In between, he warned, I would find nothing. No water, no fodder. However, he had a plan.

Before my arrival in Chile, he had contacted General Cesar Mendoza, head of the Military Police and a member of the Junta Government, and had asked him for help with my expedition. General Mendoza, who was a great horselover and had once jumped for Chile in the Olympic Games, had been very enthusiastic indeed about my proposed journey and had ordered that his carabineros help in any way possible. The desert police were prepared to assist me by arranging to supply me with hay and water at rendezvous along the way.

This was wonderful news. Nevertheless, I could not help recalling all the stories I had seen on television and in the popular press in Europe about the alleged brutality of Chile's powerful Military Police. I hoped the slight trepidation I felt at Thursday's arrangements did not show. However, when I finally met my first carabinero in his office that afternoon he seemed a mild-mannered, helpful man and began outlining a possible route for me with great efficiency. 'Our uniform', he told me, with Thursday translating, 'is the only green you'll see in the Atacama for nearly a thousand kilometres.' He added that the old mining tracks were strewn with the bones of mules who had died while carrying minerals to Antofagasta.

I had my route; I now needed my horses. Their home, San Fernando in Central Chile, was nearly 1500 kilometres away.

Next morning, when I arrived at his office, Thursday had Señor Germán Claro Lira on the telephone line. I could see from Thursday's face that the news was bad. The cost of sending the horses up to Antofagasta by lorry would be exactly 70,000 pesos, nearly £700. Germán Claro Lira's voice, speaking in soft cultured English, sounded regretful as he explained that this expense was due to the fact that no other horses or livestock would be heading for Antofagasta in the near future and so the Aculeon horses had to have a lorry all to themselves.

I was stunned. Seven hundred pounds was almost a quarter of my whole remaining budget. I could have bought two horses for far less. But what horses? The only ones in Antofagasta were some highly bred horses stabled at the small riding club. They would never survive a journey like the one I had planned. They had probably never spent even one night out in the desert. I thought back to all I had been told about Aculeon horses, their strength, their stamina, their record as warhorses. To have the right horses was the most important thing of all. Other things I could do without or economize on. I had to have them. I heard myself ask Señor Claro Lira to please send them as soon as possible.

Meanwhile I set about getting everything as well organized as I could. There really is no such thing as a solo expedition; over the next two days many people, through the help they gave, became forever part of it. Compensation for the worry about having to cash so much money was that the bank manager, Don Paricio, turned out to be a keen member of the riding club, and arranged a supply of hay for the journey which was worth more to me than anything kept in his vaults. He also said the horses could stay at the club when they arrived. An American family, based with a mining and construction company in Antofagasta, gave me advice and moral support. They also made up two long iron stakes with loops welded at their tops. The idea that I could bury these at night and tie the horses to the loops was a good one, since

32

My first meeting with Hornero and Jolgorio.

Setting off into the Atacama.

The occasional telegraph pole was a vital hitching post.

A hay drop in the desert, courtesy of the carabineros.

there certainly would be no trees to secure them to on the trail.

Most valuable of all perhaps was the gift of peace and privacy given to me by a very kind Danish lady professor called Bente Bittman, who worked at the Archaeological Department of Antofagasta's Universidad del Norte. Somehow she lived in two flats instead of one and handed me the keys to the lower one. There the mountain of my equipment was spread out all over the floor. I supplemented it by purchasing a sombrero, much more rope and some hideous purple water-carriers and tried to sort everything out as best as I could.

Mistakes I had made during my preparations in Wales started queuing up for recognition. To start with, I discovered that pedigree horses have a constant programme of vaccinations from birth. The Aculeon horses would have no need of the anti-tetanus vaccine or the worming paste which I had lugged out all the way from the UK. Furthermore, I discovered that all horse medicines could be bought much more cheaply out here in Chile. The same was true of my own medicines and much of my equipment, from socks to Camping Gaz cylinders. As usual the old maxim applied: 'What you need is half the equipment and twice the money!'

On Thursday 19 July, only four days after my own arrival in Antofagasta, the horses arrived by lorry, fresh from their lush fields in the south. They were so beautiful, like creatures from a child's fairy story. Aculeo Hornero stood about fourteen hands high, a classical dapple grey. He was the proudest-looking horse that I had ever seen, with a neck that arched majestically and big brown eyes peeping through a long thick fringe – as though he did not wish to look too much at an ordinary world. Aculeo Jolgorio was a little smaller. He was fatter and cheekier than Hornero, a dark bay with shining highlights. He immediately decided to find out if the Atacama would be any good for a backscratch. The pair had arrived complete with their own beautiful pedigree papers showing their lineage back several generations.

Both horses viewed their new surroundings with considerable mistrust, despite the relative comfort of the hospitality offered them by the riding club. In particular they seemed to have great doubts about me, especially when I took them for a ride to try out the packsaddle. Despite being tied on with reams of rope to supplement the large girth which went round outside the packs to keep them in place, everything kept falling off.

The horses were very lively and seemed determined to run away with me as often as possible. I felt that their one idea was to get away from this terrible place, and from me, and gallop off back to the sanity of their hacienda home.

Hornero would have nothing to do with the packsaddle at all. Jolgorio was a little more patient. As I experimented I finally worked out the idea of hanging the rucksack straps on the horns of the packsaddle so that one soft-framed Karrimor hung down each side. The real problems came with the water-carriers, the typewriter, the camera, the torch, the log book, and the fodder. Heavy objects had to be kept low down, and the load had to balance. However, some things also had to be easy to get at. Reaching a compromise between these two objectives was most difficult.

I soon decided that more than a certain amount of practising was a waste of time. Too many dress rehearsals and I would end up doing some damage to the horses, the equipment, or to myself before I even set off. The only way I would learn how to handle life on the desert tracks with my horses was to go out and try it. I was also driven by the thought that I had planned the whole expedition to last only about four months, so that I would reach Cape Horn during the Southern Hemisphere summer. There was no time to be lost.

So on 22 July, just one frantic week after my arrival in Antofagasta, I set off, escorted as far as the police checkpoint at La Negra about twenty-three kilometres south by a small convoy of riding club members. The wind howling over the dunes seemed to frighten poor Hornero and Jolgorio, so did the little white shrines, monuments to sudden death along the road. Several times they bolted, accelerating from a walk to a flat gallop within seconds. It was usually some time before, red-faced from exertion and embarrassment, I managed to pull them up again. The members of the riding club hid their smiles and politely complimented me on my horsemanship. At La Negra, they wheeled their elegant English-bred horses around and headed back home.

We were alone with the desert at last. The horses began to settle down a bit, probably because they were tired. During the first few days we passed Varillas, Cerro Ventarrones, then climbed up towards Cerro de Las Tortolas – each of these names on the map turning out to be no more than empty mountainous desert.

> LOG: *Three days out of Antofagasta near Cerro de Las Tortalas*
>
> The Atacama is like the surface of the world must have been before time began. A desert by comparison with which the Sahara, where one can find an oasis, is a flower garden. Here for hundreds of miles on either side of me are mountains where nothing else is alive. There is nothing green here, not even a cactus. No birds, no animals, no insects even. Nothing except minerals which horses can't eat and bleached bones which at times I feel we might end up among.
>
> This is a strange, eerie, utterly silent place, completely empty, without atmosphere either of kindness or of malice. There is neither evil nor blessing here. Just rolling mountains which have never felt the weight of a human hut, nor the struggle of the tiniest living root growing through them.

During the days it was so hot that even my sunbloc cream dissolved. But at night there was always ice in my tent and in

35

my drinking water. I valued my thermal underwear much more than the most exotic lingerie. I shared my RoC sunbloc cream with the horses to save them getting cracked hooves and they in turn lent me their horse liniment, which did wonders for my aching arms and legs, though I am not sure if it smelt quite as good as Chanel No. 5.

The desert may be famous for mirages, but I remember the Atacama most for what it taught me about reality. While the horses slowly began to get accustomed to their new life, I spent those early days in the desert utterly exhausted from trying to cope with them and with the heat. At night I often had to sit on top of my tent for an hour's rest before summoning up one last ounce of energy to put it up. Already this was turning out to be by far the hardest adventure I had ever embarked on.

We could not travel much at night, although it would have been much more comfortable to do so, for the moon – although waxing fuller every day – still set early. The horses could not see where they were going, and after dark the pits in the terrain became lethal traps.

One of my greatest problems was finding somewhere to stop. There was seldom anything to tie the horses to. Those who have been reared on Westerns where horses seem to spend most of their time hitched up outside bars, never apparently requiring food or drink, and never running away, may not be able to understand the difficulty of actually looking after two horses on the trail. Like boats, horses tend to drift away if they are not secured properly. Jolgorio and Hornero had made short work of destroying the fetters prepared for them in Antofagasta and, although we were now getting on much better together, sudden moments of fear or alarm could still make them bolt. They had to be secured. The stakes the American miners had created for me turned out to be my salvation. They worked quite well when buried deep in the sand so that the tops, with their welded loops, just showed. Good holding ground was rare, however, and I would roll a rock on the top of the stakes whenever possible. During temporary stops, for simple things like having a wee, I would simply cling on to the two headcollar ropes. I soon got tired of wearing my Welsh dungarees – the straps were too awkward.

The Chilean newspapers had been quite excited by the fact that I was a woman doing a solo expedition. I was, of course, not alone at all. I had ten feet to worry about instead of two, and three stomachs, two of them very large, to fill. Life was much harder for the horses than for myself. For a start I did not have to walk. Also I had enough cheese, biscuits, sugar and coffee to last me for weeks if necessary. My water problems too were minor compared to those of the poor horses. Best of all I was fairly free from mental stress. I kept telling myself that I was here in the desert by choice and not by accident. I was fulfilling a dream. I also tried to heed a lesson I had learnt long ago, which, in essence, is that when in difficult situations, you have to be as kind to yourself as possible.

As we travelled along I kept the same vigilant eye on myself as I did on the horses. I tried always to rest for a few minutes before I felt too tired; to drink a little water before I felt too thirsty; never to pass a rock which threw some shade without making use of it in order to stop and check the packs or make other little adjustments; to wear long-sleeved clothes which gave me a sort of mobile shelter, and to wear some form of hat, usually my sombrero. At first not just my legs and back, but my whole body had ached intolerably. One certainty is that women's libbers – of whom I am not one – who believe in burning their bras, never went joggling along ten hours a day on a very lively horse. However, the horse liniment continued to work wonders. So did walking on my own feet for about ten minutes of each hour.

As I adapted I realized I had very few real problems. My constant worry was for Hornero and Jolgorio. The people of Antofagasta had been right, of course. No one but a lunatic would go on a desert adventure using only horses. Camels or llamas yes, or better still these days, sturdy jeeps. My horses were the absolute vulnerable opposite to 'indigenous', having so many needs which this part of the Atacama could not supply at all. But then, of course, I had not planned for the desert at all; I was merely trying to get through it. I somehow had to nurse Hornero and Jolgorio to the other side of the Atacama, so that we could continue our partnership down the rest of the long, long map of Chile.

The horses themselves seemed utterly confident, against all the evidence of the empty desert, that somehow they would get enough to eat and drink. I wished I shared that confidence.

'Mules/horses require 8/10 gallons of water per day,' the *Animal Transport* manual informed me, 'and should be watered 3/4 times during the day . . . Horses/mules in work require 8 pounds of grain and 10 pounds of hay daily . . . ' Supplying such needs was almost impossible as there was no scrub or vegetation to pad out a feed. I had been unable to buy any grain or concentrate, so the horses' sole food was hay, which of course is very bulky.

In spite of Hornero's fury, I carried a bundle of hay in a large net behind the saddle. Poor Jolgorio was also loaded down with hay, as well as equipment and water, well up to the 160 pounds which is meant to be the maximum load a packhorse can carry. He kept his strength up by snatching the odd crafty bite from Hornero's net.

The bulk of the supplies and some extra water carriers had been left with the police to be dropped off at specific points on our route. They also tracked us down whenever they could to refill the purple carriers and to give us more hay. When the horses spotted the red flashing lights of the police jeep lurching across the desert towards us, they would prick up their ears and break into a trot. As long as the carabineros continued their drops, and the elements showed a similar kindness, we would make it.

As the days went by I became more and more absorbed in Hornero and Jolgorio. The two horses were completely different characters. Hornero was a proud introvert, Jolgorio an amiable extrovert. Both, however, insisted that I speak to them in Spanish. They simply would not respond at all to commands in English such as 'Stop' or 'Whoa!' Instead it had to be *'Tranquilo'*, *'Pacito'*, *'Adelante!'* or *'Quieres comer por favor, Aculeo Hornero?'* It all had to be pronounced correctly too. At first I always seemed to have my phrase book open while I spoke to them.

My Spanish was improving. Or perhaps my constant attempts to bribe them into liking me were paying off. Anyway the horses seemed to be becoming far more patient with me. This was just as well. They had a lot to put up with. I gradually developed a special routine to suit our strange life.

Our day began at around 5 a.m. when I would peer out of my tent and see the horses, bathed in orange early-morning light, waiting for their breakfast. The first job was to remove the pink Dance Centre legwarmers which I lent them to keep their legs warm during the bitter desert nights. I then took off the ponchos which I had created for them out of their saddleblankets. Then it would be time for hay and water, coffee, bread and cheese, suitably distributed, as we all three had breakfast. Their breakfast was always consumed off the 'tablecloth' of my green army rain poncho, because I had not forgotten the warning about sand in their food giving them colic.

Because they took far longer with their breakfast than I did, I would leave them in peace and set to work pulling down the tent and cramming the incredible chaos revealed beneath it into my long-suffering green rucksacks.

Stowage was much more difficult than on an ocean voyage. When 'cruising' with horses instead of with a boat, every-thing has to be completely packed and unpacked every day. And a few extra pounds seemed to make as great a difference to a horse labouring under the hot sun as to a Derby runner.

Every morning I used to sit in the sand and think: 'Is there anything in my equipment which I don't actually need?' The trail became strewn with the graves of items I had discarded and buried.

My army saucepans went. So did the chains which had come with the horses' army headcollars. So did the bottle of shampoo which some hairdressing company had kindly sent me. There was no water to wash hair with here anyway. My little Olivetti typewriter, which had also sailed the Atlantic with me, I kept as I needed it for my work. Decisions about what could be discarded were not easy. I knew that if I sacrificed that extra pair of socks, that spare torch battery, the horse-shoeing equipment or the extra emergency water-carrier, I might be sacrificing the expedition along with them.

As soon as I had packed all the rucksacks with much the same weight, it was back to the horses: to check them for any bumps or knocks during the night; to pick out their hooves and cream them, at the same time making sure that all the nails and shoes were firm. It was also vital to inspect their eyes for bits of grit or sand, and if necessary put a drop or two of Optrex in. Then they had to be groomed, to help them shed the long winter coats which caused them so much distress during the day. This task was followed by the all-important back and leg massage with liniment.

The last job was saddling up and loading the packs, still an awe-inspiring task though I was gradually using a bit more skill and a little less string! When all this was over I would clamber on board Hornero and more or less collapse in the saddle, my exhaustion telling me the day should now be over, instead of just beginning.

At midday everything would be taken off the horses again to rest their backs, and we would indulge in more hay, water, food and massage. At night, after we had camped, I would rub disinflammatory cream on the horses' shoulders and legs

– and of course, on would go the ponchos and legwarmers again. Incidentally I did keep one pair of legwarmers for myself. They were very useful indeed and did not take up much room.

The care of the horses, although time-consuming, was absolutely necessary. Hornero and Jolgorio were innocent, after all. They had not asked to come on such a ridiculous adventure. In fact, they actually seemed to enjoy all the fuss.

We had many little accidents. One of the purple water-carriers fell off and burst. The Zenith camera also suffered a fall, but survived. I lost my valuable closed-cell foam mat for putting under my sleeping-bag, and once or twice the pack slipped sideways almost bringing poor Jolgorio down with it. In general, however, we all three seemed to be coping quite well with our unusual life.

Seven nights out of Antofagasta, I settled down in my sleeping-bag feeling more optimistic than usual. Peeping out of my tent to check the horses, which I had staked to the ground, I thought they looked peaceful and incredibly beautiful silhouetted against an enormous full moon. It was a magical night – the three of us alone in the middle of what looked like a silver ocean.

'The first week,' I thought, curling up to sleep, 'the first week has to have been the hardest.' I was wrong.

Chapter Three

We were inside the mouth of some creature from a nightmare being devoured by its hot breath and sharp teeth. I grabbed for the horses and clung to them. I ripped off my shirt to put over their eyes and tried to hold their heads as close to my body as I could.

It had all happened so suddenly. I had been flung violently out of my sleeping-bag. Seconds later my tent and equipment had vanished, whipped away by the fierce wind. The Atacama was no longer a dead place. It was alive, a swirling sand dragon.

Clinging to the ropes of the horses' headcollars, remembering images of crews being lashed to the mast during storms at sea, I tied us all to a large rock which was the only solid stationary object I could see as the sandstorm raged around us. But I knew that the thin line of trust and thicker line of hemp would not last long against the plunging of the horses and the swirling of the sand. I felt we would all suffocate, that we would never get out.

'Calma . . . tranquilos . . . ,' I begged the horses, telling them that everything would be all right. They were not fooled. My nerve endings were no longer in my own skin, but under Hornero's dapple grey coat, now dark with sweat, or beneath the whites of Jolgorio's eyes. The horses were not listening to my bad Spanish, but to my feelings, my fear.

Sensing my panic, Hornero was trying to jump out of the storm up to a sky he could not see. In the darkness I saw one flash of a silver horseshoe and then, above the howl of the wind, heard the muffled thunder of hooves galloping off. The rope had snapped. My horses had gone.

I was left clutching the rock as the storm worsened, performing terrifying somersaults around me as if celebrating its success. I curled up in a ball and tried to protect myself, wincing in agony. The sand of the Atacama was not the gentle kind you find on holiday beaches, but a mixture of millions of razor-sharp pebbles and tiny stones. It stung my skin like salt in an open wound.

How long I crouched there, how long the storm lasted, I cannot say. All I know is that suddenly I was spat out of the sandworm's mouth and found myself sitting beside my rock, clutching the shreds of broken rope. It was still early morning.

I was the dishevelled centre of a jagged 360 degrees of bare horizon, where endless empty desert mountains flowed like huge seas over a solid ocean. A red round juicy sun appeared, looking too succulent for this desolation. Forty shades of purple spread slowly across the sand; then forty shades of orange and gold. It was beautiful, but its beauty was hollow. Somewhere out there were my horses.

In England a horse parted from his rider will usually make for home, but I had no home – only a tiny tent, pitched in a different part of bare desert each night and at the moment buried with all my other possessions in the sand. The horses had nowhere to make for.

I knew now that during my preparations for the journey I had been so obsessed with the icy south that I had completely underestimated the Atacama. For five hundred miles all around me there was not one blade of grass, nor a drop of natural drinking water. If I did not find my gallant little horses that day, they would suffer badly. If I did not find them the next day they would die.

I had, of course, been warned. Indeed I could have worked it out for myself. In none of the books I had consulted was

43

there any information on how to take horses through the Atacama. I had assumed that this was because it was so easy. I had looked at the map. There was a road. There were the names of places, presumably settlements of some kind.

What I did not know but had discovered in the harshest lesson I had ever had to learn, was that the road was just a road, good enough for the great desert lorries, but not for anybody to want to built a house beside it. The places were empty, with no sign of humanity, nothing more than names on the map. The reason there were no books offering guidance about how to take two horses through the Atacama was that nobody had been fool enough to try. Before me.

My little compass was still around my neck. I knew that somewhere to the west stretched the Pan American Highway. About one hundred and fifty kilometres south was the desert town of Caldera; directly to seaward, Taltal. But where were Hornero and Jolgorio? They could have run off in any direction.

Because I could not see them in the bright sun, they must by now, I thought, be over the horizon. But how far was the horizon? Fifteen miles? Twenty miles? Certainly there was no sign of the great volcano Llullaillaco, 22,065 feet high, which had been a constant presence in the first days after leaving Antofagasta.

Distances are relative, like time. When you are asleep in an aeroplane, 1000 miles can seem like one. But on our journey the last kilometre before nightfall always seemed like a hundred. As I stared at the horizon and at the savage ground beneath my feet, the distance seemed too great to measure.

I was all alone, just as I had been on my solo Atlantic crossing in little *Fiesta Girl*. But the sea, I thought, is much kinder. If you are exhausted or adrift, a current might carry you in the right direction; if you are hungry there may be fish to eat. However, there was one hard lesson I had learnt at sea, and I knew it would be the same here in the desert. You cannot afford the luxury of fear and depression in really difficult situations. You will never move quickly out of danger if paralysed by fear.

You cannot see well through the darkness of despair, or hear well against the thumping of your heart. When you are all alone you have to do the best you can; and you can never do your best if your body is quaking and you feel sick – as I did now.

I remembered the feeling from the time I thought my poor little boat was sinking in seas much too big for her; and how shaky my writing had been when later, out of danger, I wrote in my log: 'I think in difficult circumstances you just have to decide to give up fear.'

It had been so easy to write then, and was so easy to think now, but so very hard to put into practice. I prayed to God that he would not remember the times I had forgotten to thank him, and to please help me!

I had a large red cotton cloth around my head which had helped protect me during the sandstorm. Already on this journey it had served as headscarf, tablecloth, pillow, towel and a hundred other things. I tied it round my rock, so that I could recognize it again. Then, with my coil of rope and my compass, I set off. I was also clutching the horses' blue plastic drinking bowl in the hope that the call of water might be more convincing than that of my voice.

The sand from the storm, still trapped beneath my clothes, made me wish my skin did not belong to me, and the weight of the sun on my shoulders grew heavier as the temperature rose. If I looked down at my feet I felt dizzy. I had the impression that I was rushing over the desert at great speed and might lose my balance, topple and fall at any moment. In reality, of course, it was the desert itself that was moving; the surface sand was being blown past by a steady northerly wind which had risen in the aftermath of the storm.

As the hours dragged by, hundreds of horses appeared in front of me. When I got closer, some turned into hills, some into shadows, some into streaks of dust. Some just disappeared back into my mind. Every desert rock whiter than the rest looked like Hornero; every brown patch was Jolgorio. Shakespeare's Richard III never prayed so hard for a horse as I did now.

Obstinacy, I thought, certainly is one of the Seven Deadly Sins. Why had I disregarded all the warnings not to try and ride through the desert? Why had I come to Chile at all?

My feet were bleeding and my head was beginning to spin. I was so preoccupied with self-recrimination that I scarcely noticed that far away in the distance something was moving.

I hardly dared to believe it. That day too many horses had turned into shadows and rocks.

But now I saw a thin streak of dust. And it really did turn into a horse!

My eyes smarted and stung as I struggled to gaze into the glare, just to make quite sure. Yes, it was really Hornero, almost white against the desert, followed a short distance behind by Jolgorio. 'Back from the brink,' I thought. Suddenly I felt so weak with relief that I could hardly stand, but our ordeal was still far from over.

Hour after hour I struggled on behind the horses. I was no longer following any compass course, merely trying to keep my aching eyes on the shapes of Hornero and Jolgorio. They never seemed to get any closer. They kept appearing and disappearing.

At least they were apparently unharmed. They had not suffered any serious injury, as I had feared they might, during their mad flight from the storm.

But my initial relief at finding them was now replaced by an even greater despair. Every time I got close they just tossed their heads and galloped away. But not far. Perhaps they too were feeling the heat; maybe I was stumbling after them so slowly that they did not feel threatened.

Now that the panic of the storm was over, they seemed to think it all a game. Jolgorio, who loved a good backscratch, kept stopping to roll in the sand. He was no longer dark bay.

He was the colour of the desert, his mane, tail and eyelashes ferned with sand. Those eyes looked at me with amused curiosity.

The horses would survive longer than me I knew, but in the end we all three would die. Never mind speaking to them in their native Spanish; never mind phrase books. They seemed to be constantly communicating with each other in a secret language for which there will never be any dictionaries.

If only they could understand that our only hope of survival lay in my getting on Hornero's back and riding south. They looked so beautiful, tossing their tails as they played in the golden desert. If only they could realize the terrible danger we were in.

My tongue seemed to fill my whole head. My feet were swollen, throbbing and very painful. After a desperate struggle I managed to hack my boots off with a stone and walked on in socks dyed a delicate rose colour from the cuts on my heels. Still the horses would not wait.

I was shivering, even though the afternoon sun was still very hot. I longed for my tent, and especially for my small canteen of emergency water which I hoped might still be intact under the sand. Why hadn't I brought it?

With hindsight I am glad that logic forsakes us sometimes. Because logically the sensible thing to have done would have been to have left the horses while I still had the strength and made my way west alone to find the road and help. But I knew that if I left them now I would never see them again. The whole dream would die. The expedition would be over, aborted before it had properly begun. But more important, Hornero and Jolgorio would die. It would be my fault. My responsibility. I knew I did not have the courage to bear the shame I would feel.

It was late afternoon before Hornero finally stood warily still. Slowly, with my heart pounding, I inched my way towards him. He looked like a horse under spring tension,

47

wound up to explode any minute. Nearer and nearer I got. I reached out to touch him, and immediately he was five hundred yards away, snorting nervously. Next time, he allowed me to stroke him, to tickle the special part of his neck near his ears as I knew he loved. Gently I slipped the rope over his head and tied a clove hitch in his mouth instead of a bit.

Now I had to mount him. The rope really did not give much security. I knew I did not have the strength to hold him if he decided to make off again. If he was going to run away again I was determined to go with him. I led him to a mound of sand, thankful he was only about fourteen hands high; but he seemed huge as I struggled to clamber onto his back. I jumped and was astride him. The first sensation was the delicious relief to my feet.

Jolgorio, of course, was not far off. He was looking forlorn. The only reason that he had stopped was that the rope trailing from his halter had got caught under his off hind fetlock. I could see he had a nasty rope burn.

I do not think that even the sight of Ambrose Lighthouse outside New York Harbour after my seventy-day solo voyage from Wales gave me more pleasure than that of my red cloth, sighted just before dusk on a rough reverse compass course. Working out the compass variation in the Atacama had been a bit haphazard, but as at sea, my simple navigation had actually worked.

Scrabbling in the sand near the rock I found my tent and most of the other equipment, apparently undamaged. Even the typewriter seemed to be still operational. I unearthed my veterinary pack and put a little antibiotic powder on Jolgorio's foot.

I also found my emergency hay and water supply for the horses, although some of the hay had gone. I thanked God for my special hay-net which, having been reinforced en route with reams of dental floss, had actually kept some supper intact for the horses. The only thing I could not find

Household on horseback.

Arriving at Hacienda Los Lingues in September 1984.

A roadside snack.

Crossing Lago General Carrera.

any sign of was my own store of food. I drank a little water and chewed some strands of hay.

And all the time I felt an overwhelming fear that I would lose the horses and everything I had, all over again. Not because of another sandstorm, but because of a dizziness I could not control. I felt weak and nauseous and could feel my strength draining away. The horses watched me while they chewed their hay, concern – or so I imagined – in their big eyes.

I had to get some more strength from somewhere. Half-bemused, I reached for the vitamins and, scarcely realizing that they were veterinary supplies, gave myself an injection following the technique once shown me by a friendly Pembrokeshire nurse.

Suddenly I felt much worse and realized I had made the greatest mistake of all.

Then everything went black.

Chapter Four

At first I thought I was safe at home in bed in Wales. I felt comfortable, relaxed and very happy, though somebody seemed to be breathing over me, which was strange.

It was some time before, in the moonlight, I saw the shape of a horse standing close to me. His breath, which had roused me, was like thick steam in the bitter cold of the desert night. Suddenly I realized where I was and knew that I had to fight this false comfort. I sat up and struggled towards my tent and sleeping-bag.

It is difficult to feel enough confidence to allow yourself to go to sleep when you have recently been unconscious. But when I woke the next morning I felt better. I did not even feel hungry any more. My dizziness had given way to happy light-headedness.

A feeling of elation surged through me as I remembered how the horses had waited for me as I had lain helpless, followed by horrible memories of the sandstorm and my stupid mistake with the vitamin injection.

I hadn't blown it after all. We could still go on. My throat was so dry that all that I could do was to croak, but inside I was singing and cheering. Then I saw the festering rope burn on Jolgorio's foot and the gravity of our situation came back to me.

One feels a special kind of hopelessness when a horse gets ill. History is full of human heroes who, despite being badly wounded, have carried on struggling for some special cause.

Horses, however, are blessedly innocent of causes.

This horse would have to manage somehow though. We could not just stay here in the middle of empty desert, with no food, no water and not a stick of shelter.

The Atacama is not wide like the Sahara. But it was living up to its description as 'the harshest, driest desert in the world'. 'As long, narrow and treacherous as a snake,' I thought.

But that very narrowness might save us. I could not really be all that far from help. Somewhere between the mountains and the sea would be the road.

I loaded half the packs on Hornero, in spite of his objections, and half on myself. At least the Karrimor rucksacks had actually been designed for humans. Then I got out my faithful compass and set a westward course.

By midday the sand had given way to a high plateau crowded with strange black rocks shaped like tombstones. They seemed ominous as we struggled to find a way through.

It was almost dusk by the time we found the highway. It seemed totally deserted. I could see nothing but endless miles of empty tarmac stretching into the distance. I was just about to pitch the tent near the side of the road and settle down for a long wait, when I heard the sound of an engine. A little later an enormous desert lorry roared past, close enough to singe the horses' tails with its exhaust pipe. The driver pulled up a little way ahead and several people jumped out, looking very surprised to see us.

I found I was shaking all over. It was like encountering a tanker in the middle of an ocean voyage. The driver and his friends spoke some strange dialect and I could not understand a word, but they were very kind and provided both the horses and myself with water. It was faintly tainted with petrol, but very, very delicious.

About an hour later the carabineros arrived in their magnificent desert jeep. They looked very worried. 'Señor Jelvez has been asking after you,' they said. 'We have been extremely concerned . . . '

After a quick look at me, they drove off again, returning some time later with a carabinero doctor, who promptly insisted I eat a tin of what looked like babyfood. He stuck disinfectant and sticky plaster on all my cuts and bruises he could see. The carabineros also brought a very charming vet called Julio to look at the horses. 'You must come to Taltal and rest for a few days,' he insisted. 'It isn't far.'

Amid the relief came a new rush of despair. Taltal lay beyond the desert airstrip of Breas, at the end of a twenty-kilometre branch of the road. This wasn't far, but it was in the wrong direction. The thought of going backwards was very depressing. Besides, I didn't think Jolgorio could walk another step in any direction just now. 'Don't worry,' Julio said kindly, 'I am arranging an ambulance for him.' Some time later a rickety-looking trailer arrived. Jolgorio took an instant dislike to it, but eventually I coaxed both horses on board and we set off. Soon the road plunged down from the high shimmering surface of the desert to the coast.

The old mining town of Taltal seemed to lie underneath the Atacama; its outskirts were guarded by rocks, veiled in thick sea mists and smells. It was a friendly town with ramshackle wooden houses leaning carelessly sideways and, by contrast, a beautiful, well ordered plaza, full of exotic scented plants won from the desert with very great care and very little fertile earth and water.

Julio took the horses to the police station where they shared a bountiful supply of hay with four ancient and crotchety police horses. His immediate concern was for Jolgorio. 'You can buy a new engine or exhaust pipe for a car,' he pointed out. 'You cannot buy another foot for a horse, and without a healthy foot you have no horse.' He gave me a list of fresh local remedies that I could purchase at the local pharmacy.

There was a queue of mothers wanting tonic formulas for their babies, and a kaleidoscope of remedies for other members of the family. They chatted to me in a friendly way and asked me how my child was doing. They looked somewhat surprised when I explained that my patient was a horse.

Under Julio's devoted care Jolgorio recovered rapidly. We changed his and Hornero's shoes, the old ones being worn down after just over a week's walking from Antofagasta. Julio showed me how if you sharpen the tips of the horseshoe nails and bend them outwards slightly before hammering them in, they are more likely to come out easily at the right place on the hoof and not cause internal damage. It was good advice, especially as Chilean horses have a very thin horn to their hooves.

Soon we were ready to get under way again. I wished I did not feel so uneasy. Safe in the sanctuary of Taltal, I wondered if I could be ruthless enough to drive the horses and myself through the Atacama for another two weeks or more. But then I reminded myself that I wasn't just in this for myself. I had a job to do and I'd better get on with it because the weight of the faith the publishers and a few other people had in me to complete the journey successfully was something little Jolgorio would never be able to carry for me.

Another thought struck me. It was a bit like being in the middle of an ocean voyage. We couldn't very well stay where we were forever, and going back would probably be just as difficult as going on.

The deep brown stain of permanganate of potash, used for bathing the rope burn, had leaked through the holes of my rubber gauntlets. So when the time came to say goodbye to the local chief of police, Julio's wife lent me her white gloves. In Taltal, as in Antofagasta, I experienced the overwhelming kindness of the Chilean people. Wherever I went and whatever ordeals lay ahead, I felt sure that one of the hardest parts of this expedition would be the task of saying 'thank you' adequately.

On the trail again, fitter and a little better organized, we slowly returned to the strange nomadic life which had been so drastically interrupted by the sandstorm. I felt rather ashamed of my initial trepidation about the carabineros. Not only had they rescued us and put all ten feet back on the trail again, but they had kept faith with me regarding the vital hay drops. They had not just forgotten all about me after a day or so, as I had feared they might.

South of Taltal, our route took us inland back up onto the high surface of the desert, through a seemingly endless series of plateaux supported by low hills. Our slow speed imposed a dreadful sameness on the terrain. I found it hard to concentrate on any goal further away than an hour's ride. The thought that I was on my way back to Cape Horn seemed absurd. The icy seas of the south were surely as much of a mirage as the glittering lakes I saw constantly above the desert's surface. I knew that eventually we must get through it, but sometimes it seemed as if the whole world was desert.

It was a relief at last to reach the small desert port of Chañaral. Picturesque fishing boats and wheeling grey gulls uttering strange chuckling cries signalled that, in stark contrast to the lifelessness of the desert all around, the sea here teemed with fish. I ate delicious conger-eel soup, a speciality of the region, but the horses did not fare so well as the hay had not arrived. I felt an extraordinary degree of guilt at being able to eat when they could not. We did not linger in Chañaral, but kept on southward, walking on and on along the beautiful beach.

It took some time to persuade the horses to go paddling as they had never been close to the sea before. They thought the waves were out to get them. Both of them kept taking mouthfuls of seawater from the little pools along the beach and then spitting them out again with much snorting and lip curling. At last I persuaded them to go right into the sea and they splashed around as if it was their element. Everything got rather wet, but it was wonderful for the horses' legs.

If paddling in the sea was a good idea, the salt we encountered in the sand was a different matter. Some of the terrain around us now was covered with what looked like patches of snow, actually a thick crust of common salt. Even when we could not see it, the desert around us was still very salty and this I knew was very bad for the horses' hooves. I was particularly worried about the poor little white hooves Jolgorio had on his back legs. White hooves are much softer than black or grey ones. He had the bad habit of dragging them when he was tired and the fronts were beginning to look as though they had been sawn through.

In Caldera I was able to buy some tar and made a tar/RoC suncream cocktail to paint on the hooves. Here for the first time I saw some irrigated fields and vineyards, but there was still no pasture for animals. 'This has been an exceptionally dry year,' everybody told me.

For the umpteenth time I thought gratefully of Mr Thursday in Antofagasta, as some carabineros arrived with another bale of hay. I was able to supplement this by buying a little straw. While I was doing this, an old man came up and pointed excitedly at the red dragon I had sewn on my jeans. This was another mining area, rich in nitrates and copper, and a hundred years ago copper used to be sent all the way back to Swansea to be smelted.

After Caldera we crossed the green valley of the Copiapó River, where some of the finest wine in Chile is made. Then were out into empty desert again, passing through the Huasco region of the Atacama.

It was now well into August, and my long long map of Chile was become dirtier and more battered. Gradually, however, by marching relentlessly for up to ten hours a day, we conquered another fold of it. I lived with sand in my toothpaste, sand in my coffee and sand in all sorts of unmentionable places on my body, even it seemed sand in my mind. But the desert now felt more like my home, and as I gained a little more fitness and strength I was able to appreciate more of its extraordinary beauty.

The nights were especially magical. The reward for struggling out of my tent to check that everything was all right, was the sheer enchantment of seeing the horses silhouetted against an enormous desert moon, peacefully resting or munching hay; just the three of us in the middle of a vast silver emptiness.

Travelling the way people used to travel, going places cars could never go, taught me many lessons. Riding all day and sleeping in my tiny igloo tent at night, I realized how protected we are in modern life by shields of convenience. If you are cold, you can just turn up the heater. If you are in pain, there are a thousand pills to take. There are even pills to cure fear. In the desert I had no such shields. In a sense I was not just making a journey two of three thousand miles down through Chile, I was going back two or three hundred years. Travelling as our ancestors travelled, every sense is stretched, pain, fear, beauty and most of all distance are all much magnified.

From a horse's back desert sunsets are not just seen with the eyes, they are felt with every part of the body. And you pay for the extra beauty you absorb, by the fact that the bitter night cold which follows them is amplified too. The penalties and the rewards for everything are much greater.

In the region of Elqui naked sand slowly gave way to areas covered with strange cacti shaped like candelabra, which grew larger and larger the further we travelled southward. A little further still and the cacti were replaced by small scrubby bushes and little tufts of vegetation, though still no trees, and we encountered the first mosquitoes and flies of the journey. Lizards were sunning themselves on the rocks, and there was quite a lot of birdlife around. We had now reached the Chilean savannah.

As I rode out of the Atacama into the valley of Coquimbo new wonders appeared. There was the excitement of the first real grass, and the wonderful sound of the horses munching it. The first cloud after the desert. The first dappled night sky with the moon behind the clouds making it exactly the colour

56

of Hornero's coat. The first little streams, the first tiny farming villages . . . .

Hornero and Jolgorio were very excited by all these signs of life. At last there were some other people, and some other animals around. If anything, the horses viewed the first signs of civilization with far too much relish. One evening Jolgorio ate the greater part of a tarcoated telegraph pole he was tied to. I got very worried about this until I remembered that his ancestors had survived the voyage out from Spain by eating bits of the pitch pine vessels they were shipped in.

Just before we reached La Serena, he had an even worse gastronomic disaster. We had arrived at a tiny *posada* restaurant. The whole family rushed out to greet us and the señora invited me in while her children ushered the horses towards the shade of one of the first trees they had seen for a long time. It was an especially beautiful flowering tree, obviously nurtured with all the care and scarce water the family could muster. Amid the general excitement, I forgot about Jolgorio's appetite!

The distance by road from Antofagasta to La Serena is only about 850 kilometres or three days' run in a car. It had taken us more than three weeks. Because of my solitude, crossing the Atacama had been an intense personal experience. The desert's greatest gift to me, however, was that it had somehow put a whole new perspective on the adventure. Everything ahead now seemed almost unbearably rich, sharp and tantalizing.

Chapter Five

To ride on horseback through a desert carrying a typewriter is eccentric and difficult enough. Actually typing while galloping along the plain is something which even John Wayne with his reins in his teeth might have found impossible. So in La Serena I exchanged one of my precious traveller's cheques for a tiny tape-recorder on which to record my verbal log.

The horses did not think much of the idea. When they first heard me speaking English to the machine, they were so startled that they tried to run away. The Chilean countryfolk, who seemed to have a special tolerance for imbeciles and acts of God, smiled warmly as I passed.

The days were now getting dramatically cooler and the nights warmer. The horses' ponchos and legwarmers were now a thing of the past. So were the obsessive massages with liniment. I now managed to get enough water to bathe their backs and legs each evening. There was an extra hour of daylight each morning and, best of all, though the vegetation at times was still fairly sparse, I no longer had the constant worry of trying to get to the rendezvous on time for hay and water.

The next part of the expedition promised to be less one of sheer survival and more one of discovery. I was amazed how fast everything changed, even though I was riding so slowly. Every few miles further south the smells in the air seemed different; so did the sounds, the shapes of the hills and the colours of the landscape. I began to revel in the intimacy of my way of travelling. On a horse you have to cover every inch of the land, and the miracles are little ones.

We arrived at the tiny village of El Peñón in the dark and I put up the tent surrounded by a circle of about two hundred children, who all wanted to hold my torch and help. I tried to explain that my tent had been '*mi casa del desierto*' or 'my house of the desert' and it was my Chilean homestead. Anyway, how could I possibly physically sleep at all of their homes?

'*Soy perrita*,' I said, 'I am a little dog, accustomed to sleeping out of doors all the time . . . '

The truth was that I had grown to love the sounds of the night and the feel of the cool earth directly beneath me. Most of all I had become accustomed to sleeping close to my horses.

'*Hola gringa!*' they cried. 'Then we shall have a fiesta in this *casa del desierto* of yours!' And soon they were back with wine, fruit, cheese and *empanadas*. The latter are a sort of Chilean Cornish pasty and can be eaten with the hands.

As many people as possible crammed into my igloo. The rest sat on blankets outside. Somebody brought a guitar and everybody sang. Then two children got up and danced a traditional dance with much twirling of handkerchiefs.

Superficial loneliness would have been impossible while with these friendly people. But somehow, in spite of all the fun, I felt sad and homesick in a way I never had during my weeks alone in the Atacama. As the music played, I felt almost overwhelmed by loneliness. I still had such a very long way to go and though I expected my journey to take about four months, I really had no idea when I should be back in Wales. 'What this expedition is really costing,' I thought morbidly, 'is time away from those I love at home – and it can never be paid back.'

Next day, as I left El Peñón in the early morning, the first edges of the light turned the mysterious shapes and shadows of the night-time village into real houses and buildings.

I had planned what I thought would be a short cut to the next tiny village, which was called Higueritas. Instead, Hornero, Jolgorio and I found ourselves climbing a mountain. Even the lesser mountains in this part of Chile seemed fierce and steep, and this was no exception. Every now and again we came to cracks about four feet wide, which we had to jump. 'They're only as wide as little ditches,' I told myself, as Hornero and Jolgorio leapt across packs and all. The only problem was that these 'ditches' had no bottom. The cracks, probably caused by earthquakes, plunged down to deep ravines with low clouds of white vapour curling into them.

On the other side of the mountain we were greeted by an old man and his wife, who seemed to live amidst a blaze of orange mountain flowers. I was offered a poached egg and some delicious bread hot from an oven which was no more than a pile of hot sand under an open fire. The old man admired Hornero and Jolgorio who were nibbling at the green edges of a precipice falling sheer to the valley far below, and then took me off to meet his herd of sleek goats, his hens, and some rather angry-looking geese.

He had come here twenty-five years ago from Santiago, he said, where he had earned his living as a cobbler. No, he had no wish to go back. *'Porqué?'* he asked. 'I have everything here.'

He picked up a small piece of firewood and within a few minutes had carved a perfect miniature of a traditional Chilean stirrup. This he gave me, and in return I left my latest sombrero hanging in his shack.

We stumbled on down the mountainside, via a riverbed which even the water had given up as being too difficult, and which eventually betrayed us by leading us into a maze of impenetrable thorn bushes. It took several hours to get round.

The small *posada* in Higueritas was a rickety wooden

building which looked as though it did not have much confidence in itself. The most indescribably delicious cooking smells lured me helplessly towards the ramshackle door. This was not a night for my battered and gallant Camping Gaz stove, which had served me so well in the desert.

'*Sí, sí, Señorita,*' cried a large and cheerful lady. 'Of course you may camp in the courtyard.' So I organized my canvas household and the horses, and then, leaving Hornero and Jolgorio sharing a feed of maize with a flock of enthusiastic hens, I went in to supper. The señora beamed, and began ladling casserole out of a black pot huge enough to curl up in. She also served me a small glass of colourless liquid, which looked just like water and cost about the same as Coca-Cola. At the first sip flames exploded down my throat. The señora beamed even more. This was my introduction to aguardiente, distilled from the local grapes and 50 per cent proof alcohol.

I went to sleep that night with two images in my mind. That of the old man who lived with his wife and his goats among the flowers on the mountain. And that of a youth who had passed me earlier in the day. He had been galloping a white pony, a twine rein in one hand – with which he controlled the horse perfectly – and a gallon jug of local wine in the other. The boy's trousers had been more hole than trouser, yet you could not have called him poor.

The Río Limarí had flooded badly the previous month, I was told, and some of the houses by its banks were still leaning on the elbows of their roofs, one wall down. Now the whole area was very dry again and the river had skulked so deep as to be almost underneath its own bed, so I rode along its course. From time to time I would leave the horses and set off on excursions to get water, clutching the faithful remaining water-carrier and armed with my machete to cut my way through the forests of tall thistles which lined the banks.

I came back from one of these journeys to find a magnificent personage, clad in flowing poncho, high sombrero and

61

enormous glittering spurs, looking at my horses. He was bending over, examining the brandmark on Jolgorio's left shoulder.

'What?' he asked. 'Why is such a noble Aculeon horse carrying a packsaddle?'

He seemed amazed when I told him.

'What you must do,' he pronounced, 'is visit my cousin Mariano. He is a great champion of the rodeo and I think he speaks a little English. He will explain about the *media luna . . .* '

'*Gracias*,' I murmured, to show that I could speak *some* Spanish!

Mariano's farm was about eleven miles outside Socos. He immediately won my heart by ushering the horses into a wonderful field covered with thick green alfalfa. Tall and well-built, with wings of grey hair and flashing eyes, Mariano had the same charismatic personality as his cousin. Every corner of his house was dedicated to souvenirs from the *media luna*, the Chilean rodeo, which was his passion. It is called the *media luna*, he explained, because it takes place in an oval arena divided lengthways by a fence forming a half moon.

Lassoes are not used in the Chilean rodeo, he told me, but a very high standard of controlled horsemanship is. During the contest, the bullock, after being driven round the circuit, is pinned against a padded section of the outer wall by one rider and turned around by another. Points are awarded for the contestants' expertise. But these special methods are used not just in competition, but in the general herding of livestock.

The horses that perform at the *media luna* are all thoroughbreds. You can tell them because they have the year of their birth branded on their left shoulder. It is done very delicately so as not to mark their beauty, and usually can only be seen after dampening the area first. This, together with the horse's line brand, such as 'Aculeo' which comprises an A over a V, on the left flank, forms his passport for life. Such a horse is very highly esteemed and his education is not considered complete until he is at least five years old, by which time he is very highly trained.

In one classical test, Mariano went on to tell me, a poncho is thrown on the ground and the horse is brought up standing from a full gallop, with all his four feet on the cloth.

Mariano would not let me go until he had trimmed Hornero's and Jolgorio's manes. He explained that Chilean horses all have the same special haircut. The forelock and the part near the withers is never touched, but the hair in between has to be kept carefully tonsured. It is considered very bad form for a Chilean horse to be anything less than immaculate. Out of shame I trimmed my own split ends as well.

We marched all next day into the teeth of a southerly wind, which seemed to have enough power in it to have come all the way up from Cape Horn. At last, near Punta Gruesa, we found the shelter of a derelict building.

It was enough to give any English horse-owner night-mares, with sharp iron spikes sticking out of the crumbling walls, and the floor strewn with bits of barbed wire, lumps of iron and the remnants of a dozen Coca-Cola tins. I set to, hammering anything that was sticking out back flat against the wall and picking things up. After about an hour's house-work, it was habitable enough to give the three of us shelter.

All night long, everything shook and roared and as I soothed the trembling horses I fancied I saw lights out to seaward. I thought about Drake, Hawkins, Cumberland and the other English and French sailors who had raided this part of the Pacific coast in the seventeenth century, making life very hard indeed for the settlers.

The next morning was calm and sunny, as if the gale the night before had never happened. The surface of the sea was like blue silk, and in the distance the Andes wore peachy veils of mist. It was as though nature was having a fiesta and the whole countryside had been carefully polished to bring out its colours. It was far too beautiful a day to travel far.

It was five weeks since we had left Antofagasta. We had covered nearly a thousand kilometres, travelling constantly. So far the journey had been an obsessional migration southward. I had planned to take about four months to reach my goal, so that I would arrive at Cape Horn during the southern summer. But now I thought again. 'Hey,' I said to myself. 'What are you doing? What are you missing?' So I took a little turning left, and then another, ending up in small wood, where to the horses' great delight we found a stream.

It was a wonderful luxury to put up the tent in the daylight, at leisure. I unpacked everything, first the food store – my faithful trio of coffee, sugar and salt jars; the cheese wrapped in muslin; my swag bag of bread lightly coated in sugar to keep it fresh; the fresh eggs nestling among my socks. I took everything out of the rucksacks, and peeled off my clothes. Then I leapt into the stream with all the dirty clothes, thumping them on the stones to get them clean and glorying in the solitude and the crystal water.

I hung the washing on the trees around the tent, boiled a pot of coffee and fried some eggs. It was wonderful.

I drifted through the rest of the day, gathering bamboo leaves and other fodder for the horses, making small repairs – and trying to catch the croaks of the frogs and the songs of the birds on my tape-recorder.

As it grew dark I said goodnight to the horses, who were tethered beside a huge pile of fresh bamboo leaves, then retired to the tent to write up my notes. I have always liked working at night, welcoming the extra hours which few people ever seem to count. Eventually I snuffed out the candle and fell asleep feeling very content. It had been a lovely day.

It is surprising how rapidly a feeling of peace can change into one of pure terror.

Waking up suddenly in the middle of the night, I became

aware that the horses and I were no longer alone. The warning was nothing much. Just the scuffle of some leaves and the snap of a twig or two: small sounds out of sequence with the ordinary noises of the night.

I sat up, rigid, listening. A chill rippled down my back into the depths of the warm sleeping-bag. Somebody, or something, was moving in the bushes near the tent.

It was no use pretending that the desert had taught me how to control fear. Whatever it was was getting nearer and nearer. I could hear the horses, tethered on the other side of the tent, away from the direction of the noise, becoming restless.

I felt numb, incapable of action. I prayed that whatever it was would go away by itself, while I sat still in my tent. It did not.

Before setting off on this expedition, I had been advised to study judo, or better still to take a gun. I had done neither. Mine was to be a simple journey, based on mutual trust. It would be ruined if I had to go around everywhere in a defensive attitude or armed to the teeth. The general conduct and incredible kindness shown me by the Chileans ever since I had arrived in their country confirmed that I had made the right decision. Until now.

The noise in the bushes could not be ignored. I had to do something. But what? I did not feel I could just cry out something like, 'Hi! *Hola! Hey!*', the Spanish equivalent of 'Who goes there?' But neither did I feel capable of dashing out of my tent and catching whatever it was.

I shone my torch towards the horses. Hornero was wrinkling up his nose and snorting gently as though he had smelt something very strange. He did not seem all that frightened. After checking that both horses were all right and secure, I put out the torch again. At least the intruder would not be able to see my movements.

I fumbled around in the tent until I found the heavy file from my horseshoeing kit. Then, clutching the file, and

65

gathering the last shreds of my resolve, I slowly crawled out of the tent towards the bushes.

It was a pitch black night with no moon at all.

Chapter Six

What I heard when I got closer was more like a low continuous moaning than anything else. I froze, crouching, trying to force myself to be able to see. I screwed my eyes tight shut as I had learnt to do when trying to see the horizon at night when at sea. The trick was to try to imagine something darker than actual darkness could ever be.

I could see a vague outline. Stretching my hands out, I touched something solid and warm . . . and slightly sticky. It was alive! Terrified I jerked back, my heart thudding. Then slowly, determinedly, I parted the leaves of the bushes.

Two eyes looked out. Eyes full of agony and fear. Such eyes, I thought, could not be dangerous. I switched on the torch and was taken aback by a loud scream. All my own fear was immediately replaced by the numbing shock of total surprise, and the heavy file fell from my hand. Right in the middle of the bush was a woman.

She recoiled anxiously from the light and started to rock herself, moaning. Her orange woollen skirt was rucked up right to her waist. Her hands were clutching an enormous stomach. Long, thick hair cascaded in all directions, so entangled with leaves that it was hard to believe that the hair itself did not grow from the bush. She looked at me pleadingly, blinking. Her contorted face seemed very young, or very old, I did not know which. What there was no doubt about at all was that this woman was going to have a baby. And she definitely needed help.

'*No te pongas nerviosa . . . No tengas miedo . . .* ,' I murmured. 'Do not be anxious . . . Do not be afraid . . . ' Struggling for the right words in Spanish, I reached out for her hand.

I was already covered in scratches. So, as far as I could see, was she. What about the baby? The first thing, I decided, was to move her before it was too late.

She was only a small woman. Yet she was surprisingly heavy. How she had got into this angry fury of thorns and spiky branches, I did not know. I was afraid of hurting her by trying to drag her out. Yet something had to be done. But what – and how?

The snort of a horse reminded me that perhaps I was not quite so alone with my dilemma after all. Suddenly I thought of my green army poncho, whose only use so far had been as the horses' 'tablecloth' in the desert. It had holes all around its edges, presumably so that they could be secured to prevent the poncho flapping or flying off in a strong wind. It might save the situation. I wiped it down, lined it with a couple of saddle blankets and wrapped it around the woman.

The next task was to thread a small strong rope through as many of the holes as possible. Then, using a double sheet-bend, I attached the ends of the rope to the stout hemp cord I always carried. By this time I had Jolgorio standing by, and I tied the other end of the cord around his girth, with a piece of cotton cloth (my last handkerchief!) around the knot to stop it chafing him. Then I led him slowly away, and – as I held my breath and prayed, hoping she would not bump too much on the ground – the woman came too, scooped gently out of the thorns.

I got her into the tent and made her as comfortable as I could. With a series of frantic signs she insisted that I leave the tent flap open.

'*Fuego . . . fuego*,' she implored. Yes, of course, a fire.

She looked mistrustfully at my Camping Gaz stove, which I had lit to heat some water. '*Fuego . . . fuego . . .* ' Her eyes were on the shadows of the trees around us.

I went outside and prepared a site for a small bonfire, at what I considered a safe distance from the tent. Then I gathered bits of wood, chopping frantically with my machete. In the dark it was not the easiest of jobs. Lighting the damp sticks was even more difficult and was only achieved with the help of most of the surgical alcohol from my medical kit.

It was well worth it. The flames did more than boil the water at exceptional speed. They seemed to rebuild the woman's composure too. She sat in the open doorway of my tent rearranging her legs this way and that, and although the pains seemed worse she was smiling quite happily in between the spasms and unleashing torrents of almost incomprehensible Spanish. I discovered that her name was Maria Angelica and that she came from *población* Canela Alta. Apparently she had got caught out in the storm of the night before.

I could hardly believe what was happening. Fourteen years before, I had been in exactly the same position – worrying about a baby about to be born without medical aid. But then it had been my own child – my son Jimmy who had arrived on the lowered centre cabin of the thirty-foot catamaran *Anneliese*, with only my husband and two-year-old daughter Eve present. 'The oceans of his dark nine-month world had reached floodtide, my baby was waiting to be born . . . ,' had been the opening words of my first book, describing the experience.

The wheel had turned full circle. Now I was on the other side, and I felt much more frantic than I had then, as I struggled to remember what to do.

The general advice offered by *Reid's Nautical Almanac*, emergency medical section, had been, 'Keep calm and let nature take her course.' But what about the details? It had all been so very long ago.

Maria's composure vanished again as the pains became more acute. '*Calma . . . tranquila . . .* ,' I soothed her. I

69

moved her further into the tent, making her as comfortable as I could in a semi-sitting position with my sleeping-bag under her and with her back and head supported by the two rucksacks and as many blankets as I could find. I lit the four remaining candles from my store, to compensate for the fading torch, which in spite of having had its batteries heated up at the edge of the bonfire to stimulate them, was not much good any more. I hoped and prayed that dawn would come before the baby did. 'Let nature take its course', indeed. But what if something went wrong?

I recalled that one of the most important requisites was string. Three pieces, each about nine inches long, with which to tie the baby's cord. The trouble was I did not have any string at all. There wasn't even any dental floss left. I set to work unravelling a piece of rope until I had some thin strands of flax. Then I boiled them, and also my veterinary scissors, to sterilize them.

I considered my small store of painkillers, such as aspirin and DF 118. But I thought these might do more harm than good, having an adverse effect on the baby. So I just sat and held the woman's hands, thinking that the only live creatures I had helped to deliver in the intervening years between the birth of my own baby and that of this woman had been nine bulldog puppies, and those in circumstances much more luxurious than this!

Suddenly she gave a loud cry and the waters exploded with a force that wet everything in the tent. I looked and there at last was the very top of the baby's head. Two more contractions and more of the head came out. Things seemed to be going well, and Maria herself appeared relaxed and composed again.

Then I looked more closely and saw that the cord was squeezed tightly around the baby's neck. Its face was already turning blue.

The cord was slippery and hard to get hold of. Desperately I worked to ease it over the head. It would not give at all. It

70

was like tugging at a hangman's noose.

I think I promised God anything at this stage. The success of the expedition – anything – in return for the baby's safety.

Maria bore down again in the grip of one more tremendous contraction. I thought the power of it would turn her completely inside out. What did happen was that more of the baby's body appeared and also more of the cord. I tried again and finally I managed to ease it free of the neck. Seconds later the whole baby arrived – a future adventurer I felt sure – born slithery red and furious onto the folds of my Mountain King sleeping-bag!

I cleaned the stuff out of its eyes and mouth and tied the cord carefully in two places using a rolling hitch which would not slip. Then I cut it. I wrapped one of my shirts around the baby's legs and, holding it upside down, smacked and slapped the poor thing so vigorously that by the time I had finished it was not merely crying the way all new born babies are meant to, but bellowing.

What I handed back to her mother was a tiny, red-faced, indignant little girl. I sat back, feeling a much greater sense of achievement than when I had had a baby myself.

Soon afterwards, with one last contraction, looking ugly, dark red and huge, came the afterbirth. With that the whole drama was over. At last Maria Angelica seemed at peace.

I checked the baby again and made some sweet hot chocolate for Maria and myself. Then I fell fast asleep.

When I awoke, the birds were singing. It was dawn. Surely all that had happened had merely been a dream?

But no! I looked around. The tent was in an incredible mess, and curled up on my sleeping-bag, still sleeping peacefully, were the two new occupants, who had made their way into my life in such a dramatic way.

The previous night I had looked in vain for the lights of a house where I could find help. But the map showed that a tiny village could not be far off. I saddled Hornero and galloped off in search of assistance, leaving Jolgorio on watch. A mile or so further along the dusty track, I came upon a small collection of wooden shacks crouching beside the stream. You could hardly see the houses for the tall maize and sunflower plants that surrounded them. The village seemed utterly deserted. Even the dust lay still, subdued by the early morning dew. That was it, of course. It was still very early.

I tied up Hornero and went to investigate, knocking gently on the door of one of the nearest houses. The door was opened by an old lady. She could not have been less than eighty, yet I was almost dumbstruck by her beauty. She had high Indian cheekbones, extraordinary bright green eyes, and an almost translucent skin criss-crossed with lines and wrinkles which, far from destroying her face, seemed to enhance it, the way carving might some smooth piece of oak.

'Aah!' She had caught me staring and she smiled. '*Soy también una gringa!* I also am a gringa! It is because of . . . *mi Papá!*' She motioned me in.

'*Paciencia,*' she ordered as I tried to explain all that had happened. '*Quieres tomar mate?* Would you like some *mate?* If you do not drink *mate* first thing in the morning, the bad animal, the *venoa*, will get you!'

She cut me a slice of bread from a large loaf, almost filled a small mug with some green herb and poured in boiling water. After sampling the contents she passed the whole lot over to me, indicating that when I had taken a sip I should pass it back. She then topped it up again with more hot water and the whole process started again. It had quite a pleasant taste.

'Here is my son Juan,' she said as a little man with a smart goatee beard came and sat down beside us. He actually looked much older than her. Only then would she let me talk.

'Maria Angelica,' she pronounced, '*está una niña mala.* She is a bad girl . . . '

It had, it seemed, been the tradition for all the women of the village to have their babies at home, assisted only by their families. Now there was a new government order saying that

72

this was forbidden. Instead all expectant mothers were given a free pass on the bus to the nearest hospital, where everything was done for them.

Maria Angelica had been very nervous as they had put her on the bus to Ovalle, particularly as it had been too expensive for her friends to go with her. She must have got off and tried to make it back.

By now the whole village was awake, and a large crowd had gathered outside the old woman's door. It seemed amazing that so many people and dogs could have emerged from half a dozen little wooden shacks. What had caught their attention was Hornero's saddle, which, apart from its sheepskin and the comfortable Western-type stirrups, was English in style. 'What a wonderful saddle,' they cried. 'We have never seen a saddle like this before.'

Even when the old woman told them about Maria Angelica, they were more interested in me. 'What is your tent like?'

'Aren't they concerned about poor Maria Angelica?' I asked.

'Oh no . . . *todo va bien* . . . ' They felt sure from what I had told them that everything had gone fine.

They were not, I realized, being uncaring. Until the government edict none of them had been born with any help from a professional midwife or doctor. They didn't understand why I had thought the events of the previous night so much of a drama. And when I told them how my own son had been born on a boat without medical aid, they could not see anything unusual about it. 'A woman having a child is not sick, after all,' the old lady shrugged. 'Maria Angelica? *Vamos* – let us go and see.'

Some of the children held onto Hornero's tail. Two were perched behind me. Most of the villagers ran. Father Pablo had a mule. The old lady, whose name was Señora Eugenia, sat in a little wooden cart, to which three horses were attached by nothing more, it seemed, than bits of twine. The

73

procession set off up the track.

Music was playing when we finally arrived at my igloo. Maria had found my old tape of Strauss and was playing it on the tiny tape-recorder. She beamed at us from the open door of the tent. Inside everything had been tidied and cleaned up. Even the sleeping-bag had been carefully wiped down and hung on a tree to dry. The baby was sleeping peacefully in the fold of the top half of my scarlet velvet tracksuit. She looked like a princess.

The children ran around picking flowers and making garlands to hang around my horses' necks, and many hands helped to fold away the tent and clear up the campsite.

'*Necesitamos una fiesta,*' someone said.

The little houses may have been rather rickety, but each had a garden bursting with beans, potatoes and other vegetables. And there were fruit-trees – apple, fig and peach – all just about to burst into bud.

It was a memorable fiesta. It started with a christening in the village barn which the children insisted that even my horses attend, fresh flowers adorning their halters. They called the little girl 'Rosie', Rosita Angelica López.

'Perhaps,' said the priest, 'she will be a "*pata de perra*", which means "one with the feet of a dog", a wanderer – like you!'

Padre Pablo had a special new piece of equipment, a loud-speaker system he had brought from the city and which ran on lorry batteries. This was a suitable occasion to try it out. The guitars struck up enthusiastically. The drums sounded like thunder. Hornero broke free from the children and let fly a series of enormous bucks, scattering people and benches. I managed to get hold of him and he more or less dragged me outside, where he and Jolgorio were mollified by the huge pile of carrots and cabbage leaves which the children had gathered for them.

Two sheep had been sacrificed in honour of the event. These were roasted in several parts, each pierced with an iron stake which was plunged into the ground a few feet away from an enormous open fire. The feast was supplemented by heaps of potatoes, maize and all sorts of other vegetables, stirred into a huge casserole.

I became infected by the extraordinary passion with which the Chileans enjoyed themselves. These people were poor. As far as I know they received no welfare payments and they certainly did not have much in the way of housing or good clothes. But somehow they seemed to live like kings, bursting with gaiety, music and good food – all of which they had created for themselves, here on the edge of the mountainside. They had sunshine, clear water from the stream, and earth so rich that it grew the largest cabbages I had ever seen. Each house had a few square metres on which to keep a cow or a pig or a pony. Most of all these people had pride, which glowed like health on their faces.

How did they manage for medicines, I wondered, because in spite of the free maternity care, most of the medicines I had seen in pharmacies were very expensive. But maybe the local wine, at the equivalent of about 20 pence for an enormous bottle, is just as soothing, and has fewer side effects, than the expensive tranquillizers dished out back home.

The villagers read my thoughts. Why didn't I stay? They had a field, they said, which I could easily plough, using my two good horses. I could build a house if I wished. They would help me cut and shape the wood and plant maize. Juanito would sell me a cow and some hens in exchange for my saddle. And I would be able to drink *mate* with Señora Eugenia every morning. I could easily send for my husband and children. Also for my friends if I wished. After all, I had responsibilities here now. Little Rosita was my godchild.

I listened, bemused and – for a moment – tempted. 'I must leave at once,' I thought, 'before what they are suggesting begins to sound as sensible to me as it does to them!'

Next morning found me on the road again, travelling

south. After a gruelling but spectacular ride along a high cliff road, we arrived at the little resort and fishing town of Los Vilos. Rocky outcrops, interspersed with beaches where the sand seemed miraculously soft compared to that of the Atacama, led gently out into a bright blue sea. The many little guesthouses were still firmly shuttered, and the air was quite cold, reminding me that here in the Southern Hemisphere it was still winter.

The local chief of carabineros welcomed me warmly. The horses' owners, he said, had been enquiring about us and would be driving up to meet me that evening. The Atacama Chief of Police had also been in touch and had sent me a beautiful bronze plaque to commemorate my time in the desert. He had been much relieved to hear that we had got through.

Now, how had the last week gone? Had I had any particular adventures along the way? For some reason I did not tell him about the baby.

He was a kind, rather sentimental man, and after he had let me use the shower in the police station, he took me off to meet his wife and his child and to show me his wedding photographs. I knew that I had a powerful patron in General Mendoza and that he had instructed his men to look after me, but watching this man's wife preparing the table for lunch and remembering the young carabineros who had searched us out in the Atacama to bring hay for the horses, I was convinced that the help and friendliness these people gave me was not simply a matter of following orders.

Chapter Seven

'*Hola* Aculeo Hornero!' a rich dark voice said.

He looked a bit like Rex Harrison in *My Fair Lady*. Circles from his fat cigar widened into smoke lassoes as he greeted me. 'And *Hola* Aculeo Rosie, too,' Germán Claro Lira added, paying me the highest compliment. He reached into the boot of his silver BMW and thrust out handfuls of exhausted-looking carnations. 'Look,' he said to his son Arturo, 'when she walks away the horses try to follow her. That is a good sign . . . '

I had been a little nervous about meeting my horses' owners – rather the way some people feel about meeting their in-laws. I had often wondered what sort of people would send two valuable horses into the desert, in the care of a complete stranger, on an expedition most people thought was mad. They took me out to dinner for a long session of dreams, cognac and inch-thick steak – and I began to find out.

My journey was their odyssey too. Their faith in their horses was overwhelming. For them, my journey was a chance for Hornero and Jolgorio to step back into the hoofprints of their ancestors . . .

Afterwards they came back to my tent, long legs twisting around the small circumference of the igloo as the three of us drank local wine, passing two small glasses around.

How did I really find the horses?

'They are', I told them, 'more valiant than Black Beauty, more aristocratic then Nijinsky. Jolgorio now neighs every

77

time I sneeze!' I was slightly tipsy, and I wasn't expressing what I wanted to say. My relationship with Hornero and Jolgorio went far deeper than that. 'They are', I tried to explain, 'my best friends in the whole of South America. Their companionship is the only steady thing in my life.' Ever since the Atacama these horses and I had formed a very special bond. After all we owed each other our lives.

I got out the horses' pedigree papers so that the Claro Liras could explain them. Aculeo Jolgorio had enjoyed, it seemed, a distinguished but conventional past. Aculeo Hornero, on the other hand, had always been an impossible horse. Kept as a stallion because of his beauty, the most experienced *huasos* (cowboys) had tried to train him and had failed. In the end they had just given up and had sent him out to the mountain-side. Nothing could be done with him.

At last, when Hornero was aged about eight, they had brought him in again, gelded him and tried again. They had worked him continually, because only when he'd been extremely tired had they been able to restrain his wildness. Eventually he had settled down a little. In his wild early life he had built up formidable muscles and that was why he had been chosen to take part in my adventure. Unlike Jolgorio, who loved everybody, Hornero was still very choosy when it came to people. I felt stupidly proud when I heard this.

Hacienda Los Lingues, the Claro Liras' – and the horses' – home, was to be the first stopover of the expedition. Once this had seemed like a faraway dream, but now it was just three hundred kilometres to the south.

'Well, that will only take you about a week,' cried Arturo, who had worked out that while in the desert the horses and I had often marched more than fifty kilometres a day.

I planned a route: Zapallar, Quintero, Viña del Mar; then along the beach to Quintay, Algarrobo, Cartagena, Rocas de Santo Domingo. Then across the mountains, via the villages of San Pedro, El Manzano and Las Cabras, to Pelequén. In this way I would avoid Santiago.

Even so – after parting from my new friends – I was soon riding through the most thickly populated part of Chile I had yet seen. It was lush and green, a thousand fruit-trees and bushes just beginning to burst into bud in salute to the first hints of spring. After the desert, it was almost too rich a mixture to look at.

With the people came the questions – two questions most of all: 'Are you religious?' they asked. 'Do you believe in God?'

I tried to explain about the nights I had gone to sleep murmuring: 'Please, 'im up there, look after me and the horses tonight, even though I don't deserve it!' – and how in the morning when dawn came and all was well, I would try to remember to say: 'Thank you, 'im up there. Thank you for looking after us . . . ' I don't think real religion needs a church.

The other question, much harder to answer, was: 'Why have you left your husband and children? Why have you come to Chile alone?'

I rode along a beautiful empty beach to Quintero, where another gringo, Lord Cochrane, had once had his estate. The snowy mountains of the Cordillera stretched endlessly to the south on my left. On my right, the waves swept in onto reddish sand scattered with crystal pebbles.

My reverie was shattered by a thudding on the sand behind me. Two young carabineros, armed to the teeth, galloped up and cantered round me in circles as we plodded on. They had been sent to guard me, they said.

Hornero laid his ears back, and even Jolgorio let fly with his heels; for the first time since the desert days, my poor camera flew to the ground. Hornero and Jolgorio immediately made it clear they wanted to 'take on' the carabineros' horses. Even though they had been going for nearly six weeks and these horses were fresh from the stables, they were determined to outrun them. With my equipment clanking, we galloped across the sands, heading for Valparaíso.

Valparaíso means valley of paradise. But it is much more than that. On 26 February 1817 the Spanish brigantine *Aquila* confidently approached Valparaíso, deceived by the Spanish flag deliberately hoisted in the port. As soon as it had anchored, the Chilean authorities took possession of the 220-ton vessel. It was fitted out with sixteen cannon and put under the command of a young Irishman called Raymond Morris. Thus the Chilean Navy was born.

A year later Thomas Alexander Cochrane had arrived from England with a contract as commander of the growing Chilean fleet. Valparaíso had remained the headquarters of Chile's navy, and the midshipmen's college established there in 1818 had developed into one of the finest naval academies in the world.

In Viña del Mar we were put up at the carabineros' jumping school. It was while I was there that Arturo came to see me for the second time. He had driven up from San Fernando so fast that his car had blown up.

'It is vitally important,' he said, 'that you get to the hacienda by the 8th of September.' This was in four days' time. 'It was the only day,' he explained, 'when everybody could come.'

'Why?' I asked. What did he mean? The sinking of my heart must have shown on my face.

'If you cannot make it,' he said anxiously, 'the reception will be a great disaster for us.'

What reception?

The reception for all the people who had had faith in the project and who had helped Hornero, Jolgorio and me on our journey. Margarita Ducci, the National Director of Tourism, was coming. And Mr Thursday, all the way from Antofagasta.

I had been looking forward to easing the horses gently through the last few days before they reached the hacienda, so that they would arrive home fresh and unstrained. Jolgorio's delicate back hooves were giving trouble again.

And I was worried about Hornero's back, which had carried a saddle every day for ten hours.

But there was something about Arturo's face – his enthusiasm, his fervent faith in the horses, in the project – that made it seem important to get there in time, if we possibly could. It was a matter of honour at least to try.

I sent all Jolgorio's packs ahead. Also Hornero's saddle. Instead I rode him bareback, to spare him. And, because by now I had trained him to be guided only by voice, I removed his bridle and bit and used only a headcollar. What made the next few days more difficult was that now the carabineros rode with me all the time. In the Atacama, my attempts to spare the horses had not looked ridiculous because there had been no one to watch them. Now I felt rather stupid massaging the horses' backs and walking on my own two feet whenever I had the energy, in order to save Hornero, while the carabineros galloped around and in front of me with great enthusiasm, on fresh and spirited horses.

I would never forget their kindness to me in the Atacama. Now, however, their attentions drove me mad. Even worse, when we met people on the road, they just murmured 'Buenos días' and walked away. Or else they talked only to the carabineros and not to me.

They could not lend me other horses to spare mine, because I was pledged to use only Hornero and Jolgorio. Neither could they offer me accommodation because I always liked to sleep in my tent, close to the horses. So all they could do was to ride with me and this had already upset the fragile balance of my life on the trail.

As soon as the horses were safely back at the hacienda, I decided, I would go to Santiago to see General Mendoza. I would thank him for his help, but I would also beg him not to destroy the rest of the adventure by over-protectiveness. Kindness is sometimes the heaviest burden of all.

On 7 September, the day before the party, I had a very bad stomach ache and was in agony as Hornero bumped me up and down. I decided to stop at Pelequén, a little village a few miles north of the hacienda. 'I'll camp there and rest,' I thought. 'Then I can tidy myself and the horses and ride in reasonable style to the hacienda tomorrow for the reception.' I had never forgotten how Francis Chichester, on his round-the-world voyages, had always shaved and put on a clean shirt before arriving in port.

Almost inevitably, my plan came to nothing. In the late afternoon when we were still about seventeen kilometres from Pelequén, Germán Claro Lira arrived, beaming, in his beautiful silver car. He looked very happy and excited. 'Can you make it in time for dinner?' he asked.

'Of course,' I heard myself reply, and we trotted on. I leapt from one back to another to save each horse in turn. There was something about this man and his unshakeable confidence in his Aculeon horses!

Two hours later it was all worth it. Out of the gloom towards us came Germán on a magnificent black stallion, followed by all his horsemen, wearing scarlet ponchos and mounted on the best of his champion horses. Hornero and Jolgorio pricked their ears and took their place at the head of the procession. Hornero took a quick nip at Germán's stallion as he came alongside, just to keep him in his place.

Then the silver BMW appeared again, this time driven by Marie Elena, Germán's wife. 'Hello,' came an English voice from inside. 'Well done! We'll go on ahead to the house and pour you a whisky!' It was John Hickman, the British Ambassador to Chile and his wife Jenny. They were the first English people I had met on the whole journey. There was a lump in my throat.

Shortly afterwards the horses were led away by many caring hands to their own stables, which had their names written above the doors, and I was taken to one of the most beautiful bedrooms I had ever seen.

'No tent tonight!' said Germán, pouring the first hot bath I had had for more than a month. 'Dinner', he told me, 'will be in half an hour.'

Chapter Eight

Cut crystal glasses in place of my tin mug. Gleaming silverware instead of my bent fork. I sat there, stunned at the suddenness with which I had exchanged my tiny tent for a luxurious dining-room.

Chandeliers blazed over the antique furniture. Cognac was served in a red sitting-room, an exact replica, I was told, of one used by the Queen in Windsor Castle. Dinner itself, served on the beautiful mahogany table the Claro Lira family had used since 1800, was eaten by candlelight. But there all similarity with life in my igloo ended.

Suddenly the language barrier had gone, and I could talk English. To speak was almost frighteningly easy and yet – although I believe I never stopped talking – I could not say anything sensible at all.

My tracksuit felt gritty and slightly damp and I felt I ought to have a dust sheet under me before sitting down. My hair, too, was spiky and bleached and stuck out in all directions.

I felt alien, strange, as though I should be outside, or in the stables. Yet, at the same time I was choked with relief at having arrived at the end of the first leg of my adventure; and overcome with emotion and gratitude for the wonderful welcome I had been given. It needed all the kindly understanding of the Claro Liras and the Hickmans to steer me through the evening.

Afterwards I was shown back to my beautiful bedroom, to begin the adventure of my first night in a bed for nearly two months. The linen sheets had been neatly turned back and inside, I found a hot water bottle!

The fantasy continued next day as, with a discreet knock, the sunlight and a maid in a neat blue uniform streamed in with my breakfast: silver egg cups, hot bread rolls, coffee . . .

All the bedrooms led out onto a central patio, where delicate multi-coloured ivies laced the trunks of trees said to be up to one thousand years old, and brilliant peacocks strolled and called to each other among the rare shrubs and bushes. In the centre of this patio were wicker tables and chairs, where the Hickmans and the Claro Liras were having morning coffee. In the background all was activity. Servants were carrying more tables and chairs to the great gardens at the front of the hacienda. Others were bearing trays of champagne and the Chilean national drink of Pisco Sour.

I said good morning to my hosts, then went to see the horses. I stood for some time watching them being groomed by so many hands that I could hardly count them. Their life had changed as much as mine.

The first of the guests from Santiago was already arriving by the time I got back to my room to change – to find that all of my few clothes had been emptied out of my rucksacks and had disappeared.

'They are being washed,' I was told.

Jenny Hickman came to the rescue and salvaged my favourite yellow shirt and tracksuit bottoms, ironing them over and over again to make them dry, while the servants looked on in astonishment that an ambassador's wife should do such a thing – even for another gringa!

The slightly damp shirt clung coolly to my shoulders while the rest of the day passed in a sort of fantastical dream. Car after car swept up. The Minister of Education arrived. Then the French Ambassador. Then Margarita Ducci and her husband, and with them an overwhelming number of what seemed like the glittering élite of Santiago society. Best of all was the arrival of Mr Thursday.

'The horses do not mirror the hardships they have been through,' he said kindly, patting Hornero and Jolgorio and taking pictures to reassure their friends at the riding club in Antofagasta.

Germán had not allowed the horses to be outdone by the fashionable gathering. Hornero wore a handwoven rug that was over three hundred years old, Jolgorio a handmade cowskin headcollar. A charming lady journalist gave me a present of her sombrero and lent me her pearl necklace – so that I should fit in, she explained.

She was just one of many press and television people who had arrived with the visitors. They went around proffering enormous orange-coloured microphones which made one feel one ought to take a bite. Six gardeners put up my tent, now miraculously clean, in the front garden and the horses were photographed beside it nibbling the lawn. After lunch, we all made our way to the hacienda's *media luna*, where there was a parade of Aculeon brood mares and about two hundred of the best of the young horses, followed by a magnificent display of horsemanship with old Arturo resplendent once more in his red poncho. It was another lesson after all I had learnt from Mariano.

Don Arturo demonstrated, in abbreviated form, how the trial of a Chilean rodeo horse consists of eight complicated tests. The first, the 'walk', shows off the elegant rhythmical stride of the horse. The next consists in galloping the horse in a straight line and halting him so abruptly that his hind legs slip between his forelegs and he almost sits down like a dog (the same test described as the poncho test by Mariano). The 'Troy' test shows off the horse's agility and speed. At the gallop he must turn on one foreleg and then continue galloping in another direction. Similar to this, but more difficult, is the test where the horse must turn on a hindleg.

Then there is the 'figure of eight' where the horse must canter in a figure of eight not more than ten metres in length.

Next to be demonstrated was 'turning on the spot', where the horse has to swivel around on one hind leg and then gallop off in the opposite direction. The final test is where the horse has to stand motionless and alone at his rider's command. Don Arturo demonstrated this by dismounting and walking some distance away. The horse was still standing stock still as he came back and climbed into the saddle again. It was important, one of the other *huasos* informed me, that at this stage the horse did not arch his back as the rider's weight went on, but remained relaxed.

As suddenly as it had begun the whole pageant was over. Everybody said goodbye and the smart cars purred off back to Santiago. Servants cleared away dozens of empty champagne bottles and I went to bed more tired than after riding fifty kilometres the night before.

Yet somehow it was hard to sleep. Getting accustomed to comfort seemed just as hard as getting used to discomfort had originally been. I kept reaching out to touch the edges of my tent, finding instead what seemed like an alarming drop to the floor.

The horses did not seem to have had the same difficulty in settling into their luxurious life. They had looked so happy as I had said goodnight to them, knee-deep in beautiful deep clean straw, munching the finest alfalfa and maize.

Next morning, their own personal vet, Dr Antonio, who had known them both since foalhood, came to see them and to examine them. The scars of the journey showed only in Jolgorio's back feet, where the hooves were still worn critically short. They looked as though the fronts had been cut across with a knife. Apart from this both horses were very perky and quite fat. Even so I knew the time had come to give the horses something back for all the effort they had put into the journey. And what better place for them to have a well-deserved holiday than their own home? So they had tonic injections, anti-parasite medicine and their shoes were taken off, then they went joyously off to grass to rest and recuperate.

The next two weeks, while I waited for those precious extra inches of Jolgorio's hooves to grow, passed very quietly. I spent the mornings working on my notes at the beautiful antique table German had lent me instead of a desk. Most afternoons I would borrow a horse and ride down lanes lined with fragrant eucalyptus trees to the clover field where Jolgorio and Hornero were becoming sleeker every day. I also had time to explore the hacienda itself. It was much more than just a beautiful house, it was a fascinating lesson in history and human endeavour.

In 1540 Pedro de Valdivia, one of the conquerors of Chile, took possession of the valley of Santiago in the name of Emperor Charles V of Spain. Among the noblemen with him was General Juan Davaloz Jufré, who in 1541 was appointed the first mayor of Santiago in recognition of his services. Before the end of the sixteenth century his nephew Melchor Jufré del Aguila followed him as mayor. Well-known at the time as a writer, he was awarded the Angostura estate, of which Hacienda Los Lingues was a part, by the then King of Spain. The property was later inherited by his daughter Ana Maria del Aguila, from whose line came the Claro Liras.

Since then the sturdy red walls of the hacienda had absorbed a lot of suffering as Los Lingues had endured financial, social and physical earthquakes. There had been times when the family had been temporarily exiled. When they had returned they had mostly lived and worked in Santiago. Not so Germán. His heart was always in the country.

A pipe and a pouch of tobacco from his father and not a silver spoon had marked Germán's twenty-first birthday, and he had had to drive trucks to earn his way through university. By the early 1960s, having qualified as a civil engineer and doing well in business, he had persuaded his relations to sell him their rights in the hacienda and it was there he brought his young wife Marie Elena heavily pregnant with their first child. His mother-in-law had been horrified. There had not been one room fit to live in. No garden, no working kitchen, nothing. The hacienda was dying of neglect. Germán and Marie Elena had set to work papering the walls, redecorating, rescuing the priceless treasures. Their hearts had been there ever since.

The family's pride was that the struggle did not show. I began to understand why Hornero and Jolgorio had come into my life. The Claro Liras knew it was important to believe in dreams and ideas.

The oldest part of the hacienda was the chapel, converted from what had been a stable when the hacienda had been built around 1550. Inside was a gold altar from the Atacama culture, a Jesuit prayer bench from *c.* 1600, many rare paintings and a magnificent ivory Christ which had belonged to Pope Pius IX. Acclaimed as the biggest piece of pure ivory in Chile, it has been attributed to the sculptor Benvenuto Cellini.

The doors leading into the great drawing-room were carved by Bavarian artists brought to Chile by the Jesuits in the sixteenth century. The collection of Chinese porcelain in the red sitting-room came from the Imperial Palace in Peking. There was a pianola from the end of the eighteenth century which had been made for a princess, a collection of guns from the time of the pirates and a vast array of crystal glasses.

I had never seen such a collection of beautiful objects, but most splendid of all, to me, were the stables. When Germán and Marie Elena had rescued the hacienda's treasures, among them were the Aculeon horses. Germán had bought the exclusive right to breed the line and he and his devoted band of *huasos* had brought the horses in from the hills near the lagoon of Aculeo. He was a careful breeder, keeping only the best of this ancient line, which was why the stable office was thick with premiums and rosettes.

But before he had brought the horses, Germán had rented

a hill with a quarry producing pink marble. The result was 3500 square metres of hand-cut pink stone forming the floors of the stables, which also had their own baths, a delivery room and a laboratory.

It was not just the horses' pedigrees that Germán Claro Lira was so proud of, however. Marie Elena came from the Lyon family, descended from that of Lord Glamis of Scotland and the Earls of Strathmore, and the whole family was very proud of a letter from Lord Lyon King of Arms in Edinburgh, confirming that Marie Elena is related to the Queen Mother and thus is a distant cousin of the Queen. Germán smiled happily at the suggestion that before marrying her, perhaps he studied his wife's breeding as carefully as he might the pedigrees of his magnificent horses!

I kept my promise to myself and went to see General Mendoza in Santiago. I thanked him for all his men had done, but begged him to ask them not to pay me quite such close attention.

'We want you to succeed,' he said. 'We shall still keep an eye on you, but *a más distancia* – more at a distance . . . '

The following weekend he invited the Claro Liras and I to an exhibition of the fabulous Cuadro Verde police horses, and also to inspect his own fine-bred multi-coloured driving teams. It was plain where his heart lay.

Two weeks passed. The aches and pains I had arrived with had now been replaced by a restlessness which was even harder to bear. I had everything I could wish for. My meals were brought to me on a silver tray so as not to disturb me when I was working. I could ride any horse I wanted from the stable. I could swim in the lagoon, explore the soft green foothills of the Andes rising behind the house, I had a beautiful place to live. Yet I was not entirely happy. I was desperate to be off on my adventure again. And now that there was no longer the hardship of the trail to distract me, I suffered from acute attacks of longing for my family.

The Argentinian ambassador to Santiago and his wife

came to lunch one weekend. After we had got over the preliminary embarrassing unanswered and unasked questions about the Falkland Islands, they proved very charming and we drank a toast as the Union Jack and the blue-and-white flag of Argentina were crossed on the dining-room table. The ambassador's wife advised me to hurry back to Wales. 'Otherwise,' she said, 'you'll arrive back at your home and your family will raise their eyebrows and ask, "Who are you?" ' I was afraid she was right.

The horn on Jolgorio's white hooves grew terribly slowly. Yet it was either another inch of hoof, or another horse. I had more than sentimental reasons for not wanting to change the horses. I genuinely thought they were the best horses for the job. Not only were they used to my eccentricities and to life on the trail, but they were accustomed to walking up to ten hours a day, seven days a week, and were fitter than even the finest champion in the Aculeon stables. And because of their very different characters and their great loyalty and friendship with each other, they made a wonderful team. I would not have wanted two Jolgorios or two Horneros. But one of each was magic.

But was it fair to them?

'Don't worry,' said Germán. 'On your adventure, these horses are doing what horses were born to do. Most horses are bored.'

The approach of my birthday on 2 October concerned me, not so much because of the passing years, but because of the passing months of my adventure. Cape Horn was still a long way off.

At last the vet gave the all clear. It was time to go. I thought the first day of my new year would be a good time to start. But 'You cannot leave on your birthday, the first spring birthday of your life,' German said firmly. 'I've ordered a special dinner.'

So it was on 3 October, on a beautiful crisp morning, that I finally left the hacienda feeling better prepared than ever before. Once more I was accompanied by Germán on his favourite stallion Aculeo Impulso and the horsemen in scarlet ponchos.

As we trotted through the dusty lanes, a little calf was being born in a nearby field. We stopped to give the cow a hand. 'It must be a good omen,' said Germán, 'you'll have no more trouble on this expedition.'

A little further on Germán and his horsemen said goodbye. Hornero and Jolgorio fairly danced away. We were on our way south again at long last.

Chapter Nine

———— ❦ ————

LOG: *3 a.m.; 5 October 1985; near Curicó*
Philosophers have always debated the nature of happiness. But I would say that pure happiness is very close to what I am feeling right now. Through the open flap of my tent, a bright crescent moon shows both horses so close to me that I can almost touch them as I lie in my sleeping-bag. Mixed with the Strauss which is playing on my tape-recorder, I can hear the wonderful sound of them cropping rich grass.

I have just made myself some delicious coffee, courtesy of my Camping Gaz stove, and am drinking it by the light of a candle stuck on top of the coffee tin. My handwriting may be suffering from circumstances and each flicker of the light. But it all seems so magical I feel honour bound to record what I feel like, now . . . before I forget.

We were travelling through a rich flat valley with high mountains on either side. On my left were the Andes, my companions since Antofagasta, now capped with snow and ice. Four thousand five hundred miles long, this was not just the longest mountain range in the world, but also the youngest and most restless, with scarcely a year passing without some part being dramatically rearranged by an earthquake. The jagged young peaks seemed conscious of their heritage – born in violence and glittering in ice. It seemed incredible that such harshness should be entirely responsible for the wealth of gentle green in the valley below.

Everything here was bursting with what appeared to be the concentration of ten entire springtimes, not just one. The fruit-trees were in full blossom. On the vines, delicate green leaves were just beginning to show. Everywhere were lush fields, new lambs, sleek cattle. Pairs of oxen and horses were ploughing the rich brown earth. Everything was growing so furiously that one could almost hear it. Even the dandelions were enormous.

Every day was a feast of little happenings, little adventures: the almost unbearable suspense of wondering what might be around the next bend. Colours, shapes, buildings, landmarks would appear indistinct in the far distance, puzzling my eyes, gradually taking shape as I rode towards them. When travelling by horse there is a long time to look at something before it goes out of sight. I found myself talking to the trees, chirping to the birds in the hedgerows, even waving at the cows in the fields.

The horses also seemed to unlock all human barriers of circumstance or shyness. Progress during the next ten days, as we made our way south towards Chillán, was slow. But for once this was because of the pleasure of the journey, and because of the hundreds of people who stopped to talk to me and to pat Hornero and Jolgorio.

Everybody along the way seemed almost to be expecting us. From every little farm, children and dogs came rushing out, followed by the rest of the family. '*Quieres tomar un cafecito?*' they would ask. 'Would you like a coffee?' There followed a stream of questions, which I struggled hard to understand. Britain looked such a small island on the map that they were convinced that all British people knew each other. Most of the children were mad, it seemed, about Duran Duran, Sting, Elton John and other pop singers. Had I met them? Also did I know *El Príncipe* Charles and *La Princesa* Diana?

Near Villa Alegre we were met by the lady mayoress. We had, she told us, been challenged to take part in a race. The local horse breeders had heard all about the Aculeon line and were determined to pit their horses against mine.

We were escorted into the town, where Hornero and Jolgorio were groomed by prisoners let out of the local jail. The best thing before a race, they insisted, was half a gallon of local wine poured into the bran mash. Neither Hornero nor Jolgorio was a racehorse, but somehow it seemed a matter of honour that one of them should race. I chose Hornero because even after walking ten hours under the hot sun in the Atacama, he had still had enough edge of speed to lead the gallop away from swirling sand-ball squalls. All I had had to do was tickle a certain part of his neck and off he would go. He was also slightly faster than plump Jolgorio.

It was all over as soon as Hornero spotted the two beautiful stallions ridden by local *huasos*. Hornero hated stallions. Maybe he was just jealous. Anyway, back went his ears.

The course was eight circuits of the central plaza. The band struck up and round and round and round we went. I could feel Hornero's anger as one of the stallions dashed past on the last lap. He never had had the philosophy to be second best. I felt him push forward with one more burst of speed and I just clung on. It was pronounced that we had won by a neck.

I was gradually becoming accustomed to living out of doors again. I had paid for the weeks of luxurious comfort at the hacienda in the extra discomfort when under way again. I had lost the hard edge formed by the first part of the journey, and a lot of my precious immunity to heat and cold. I still had a sore throat and a cough which had plagued me since leaving Los Lingues. I steadfastly refused many kind offers of a bed in someone's house. If I did not manage to live in my tent now, I certainly would not cope in the wilderness of the south. I tried to keep myself and the horses on as strict a routine as possible so as not to become spoilt on this relatively easy part of the journey. I walked as much as possible to toughen myself up.

This made me very popular with the children, who in this part of Chile always seemed to be around my horses. Sometimes I was able to give as many as three of them at a time a lift on Hornero, and at midday when I stopped to rest the horses they often helped me unpack the rucksacks and shared my picnic lunch.

Molina, Talca, San Javier, Villa Alegre, Putagán, Linares, San Esteban . . . the towns and villages I passed through were mostly a few miles back from the main road. Places which few people, even Chilean visitors, ever get to see, they are protected from invasion by the outside world by the fact that they are not especially famous or beautiful. But they are where the ordinary people of Chile actually live, and give a much truer reflection of Chile, I felt sure, than Santiago with its great buildings and extremes of wealth and poverty.

I took more and more pride in my independence. Everything I needed was provided by the horses and what they carried on their backs. I had my home, my work, my transport, no worries about fuel, and for a few pesos I could buy simple delicious food from the little homesteads and towns I passed. I could go wherever I wanted and where I arrived each evening was an adventure, with the whereabouts of my camp dictated by fate and how far I had managed to get that day. Always there were surprises.

Near Villa Rosa I came back to my tent to find it seemed to have become alive. It was bending this way and that from inside. I rushed forward to investigate, then stopped, puzzled. Contented grunting noises were coming from within. For a moment I thought that the tent had been commandeered by a pair of passing lovers, but when I peeped inside, I saw – eating my bread and cheese, and investigating all my belongings – a family of five young pigs.

When I told the villagers of Villa Rosa about the pigs, they immediately offered me one as a present. 'Take him with you,' they urged. 'He'll be better than a dog as a companion – and if you get too hungry you can always eat him.' I was sceptical about my horses approving of this idea – or indeed the pig.

Many of the people I met were surprised that I did not already have a dog with me for protection. Every Chilean horseman riding through the country seemed to be accompanied by at least two. But one of the secrets of camping in open country as a woman alone, and still sleeping peacefully, was the belief that nobody could find me. I knew that the horses and I had only to go a little way off the track and put up the tent among trees or behind a rock, and it would be very difficult indeed to find the campsite after dark, especially as, in the thickly populated regions of central Chile, I never lighted an open fire. If anyone did approach, the horses' gentle restlessness would be enough to warn only me. A barking dog would be a homing beacon for any intruder.

Of course, the real reason for not having a dog – or even a pig – with me on the journey, was that I knew it would break my heart to have to part with it afterwards. Because of quarantine regulations, I would never be able to take it back to England. Already I felt anxious about the thought that one day I would have to say goodbye to Hornero and Jolgorio. Every day as I became fonder of them and taught them to have more confidence in me, I felt more unhappy at the thought that one day we would have to part. It was the price for treating them as more than mere transport.

In many ways life in the pretty agricultural village of San Gregorio could not have changed much in the last hundred years. Horses waited patiently for their owners outside the bars, and from time to time the dust of the streets would be stirred by yoked oxen pulling heavy loads. The twentieth century had arrived in the form of the smart new medical post, where I was set upon by a gleaming-eyed nurse called Elsa who pumped me full of penicillin to cure the last remnants of my sore throat.

I told her about the drama of the baby's birth in my tent. She defended the government order forbidding home births: infant mortality rates had been dramatically reduced. 'Having a baby at home is very wonderful,' she said, 'so long as all goes well . . . '

I went to sleep in my tent to the strains of music from loudspeakers hidden in the trees and when I woke at 6 a.m. what sounded like yet another enthusiastic Chilean fiesta was still in full swing, the last chords of the music mingling with the first cock crow of the morning.

The next day, 17 October, we arrived in the town of San Carlos and the spell of the last two happy weeks broke. We had been given special permission to camp in the beautiful park of the jumping stadium. It should have been an idyllic night, the sky beautiful and clear, with Orion's Belt almost leaning against the moon and Sirius, the Dog Star, dramatically bright behind.

But there was no peace. All night long there was the thudding of galloping hooves and I watched in helpless fury as my horses tried to defend themselves against the baiting attacks of three enormous alsatian dogs. Every now and again the horses would stop and turn on their attackers, striking out with hooves and teeth. Then the furious barking would disintegrate into a howl. But a little later it would all start over again. The horses were so maddened that I could not catch them, so it was impossible for us to get away. It was the only time on the adventure that I truly wished I'd had a gun.

At last dawn came and the dogs slunk away. Mercifully the horses, though highly nervous and wet with sweat, seemed otherwise unscathed. The in-calf cows in the park had not fared too well, though. Their swollen teats and udders had all been torn and bitten by the dogs.

I hated the place and all my instincts told me to leave it as soon as possible. But the horses were tired out and needed to rest for a few more hours. So I was pleased when the park-keeper told me he had arranged for the local vet to come and reshoe my horses. I decided to wait. It turned out to be one of the worst decisions of the journey.

For the moment though, all seemed well and in the afternoon we set off for Chillán where the horses had another mane trim and I was presented with a diploma by the Pinto Rodeo Club, a rare honour for a woman, since rodeo competitions are a purely male concern. The woman's part consists in balancing glamorously on the back of the winner's saddle after the event!

As the sun rose the next day, I lay in my tent near Bulnes feeling too lazy to get out of my sleeping-bag to chase away six large flies which had settled on the roof of my igloo. I was intrigued by the fact that they sat only on the white panels, deliberately, it seemed, avoiding the green. Like Robert the Bruce in his cave I felt I badly needed a spider – not just to eat the flies, but to inspire me to make the right decision.

Puerto Montt, the last town on the main body of Chile and the road and rail terminus, was now about 600 kilometres south by the most direct route. Below it lay the wilderness of the Southern Archipelago with its swamps, impenetrable forests and hundreds of uninhabited islands. It was important to reach Puerto Montt so that I could get accurate local information on the best way to get through this wilderness, and to do so while it showed its gentler summer face.

Yet the direct route to Puerto Montt was the Pan American Highway. To walk on tarmac any more than necessary seemed to negate the whole purpose of using horses instead of a car.

I decided to turn west at Bulnes, travelling to Concepción and then through the coal-mining districts of Coronel and Lota. I would then make my way south through Mapuche Indian country by the little used coastal tracks, marked on my map as unsuitable for vehicles and therefore doubly appealing.

It would not take that much longer, I decided, especially as

99

the horses and I were very fit, and everything was going so well with the expedition. It was just a matter of travelling a certain number of kilometres each day.

We arrived on the outskirts of Bulnes to be greeted by what seemed like all the taxis in the town. They formed a convoy and accompanied us, honking loudly. The Mayor explained that they were putting on a concert that evening in aid of a local charity. Would I like to sing some English songs?

Mercifully they were happy when instead I suggested a display I had taught the horses having been inspired by the Cuadro Verde police horse exhibition in Santiago. Hornero would now stand motionless while I perched upright on his bare back. Sometimes I could even perform a careful somersault as I had seen the police riders do. He would also stand still while I lay under his stomach with my eyes shut, pretending to be asleep. And if I said, 'Hornero, *levante las patitas*' or 'Please lift your feet,' he would lift up all his hooves one by one for me to clean or inspect. Jolgorio was not so teachable. While standing still, he would forget his role immediately if he suddenly spied something tempting to eat. But he had his own speciality. On command he would follow me wherever I went. I could even walk in figures of eight with my arms folded and not looking back and he would follow closely behind. If I ran he would trot, kicking his heels up out of sheer high spirits every now and again. But however fast I ran, when I stopped abruptly, he would stop too, his nose never far from the titbit in my pocket.

Our next stop, Quillón, was the heart of the wine country. But the local people did not seem to care much for their own delicious product, so freely available. Soft drinks like Coca-Cola were more expensive and fashionable. I was invited to dinner by the owners of a famous vineyard; they couldn't understand why I seemed a little disappointed when they served Fanta Orange instead of wine at the dinner table!

Ten kilometres south of Quillón the reason why the countryside was becoming greener and lusher was suddenly

100

apparent; the climate underwent a dramatic change. On 22 October, when we arrived in Florida, which was quite unlike its namesake in North America, it began to pour with rain. And it went on pouring. I swathed myself in plastic bags. Soon I felt that I and all my possessions were living inside a world made of polythene.

Stormclouds of a different kind were also gathering around the expedition. Twenty miles out from Concepción, poor Jolgorio suddenly went very lame indeed. He seemed to get worse every hour. The horn of his near front hoof became so hot it was as if it was on fire. Soon he could not put it down on the ground at all. I lurched from the exaltation of the past three idyllic weeks to total despair. Once again the carabineros came to the rescue. Appearing from nowhere, it seemed, they took my packs and we limped slowly into the sanctuary of the jumping stables in Chiguayante, just beyond Concepción.

When Erwin, the carabineros' vet, took off Jolgorio's shoes he immediately discovered the reason he was so lame. There really had been a curse on us in San Carlos. The attack by the dogs had not been the worst thing about the place. It seemed that in putting on the new shoes, the vet there had banged a nail into the sensitive part of Jolgorio's foot. That poor horse always seemed to be the one to suffer.

An anxious week passed as I helped Erwin and the two other vets who supervised the jumping stables to nurse him. Luckily, unlike Hornero who hated injections and whose favourite contact with vets was with his teeth, Jolgorio actually seemed to enjoy all the attention, and was a very good patient. He had endless antibiotic injections, disinflammatory injections, and then multivitamin injections necessary to counteract the fact that too much penicillin can give a horse anaemia. He even put up with a local injection right into the fetlock above the hoof. He improved rapidly. It was a credit to the help I received that within a week and a half the horse was one hundred per cent fit again. We could go on.

101

We never got to leave Chiguayante on 5 November as I had planned. They say pride comes before a fall. Certainly pride and showing off became my downfall. I was feeling happy and high-spirited because we would soon be on our way again. Hornero, stuffed with the finest oats, was also feeling high-spirited. He allowed me to begin our little display of horsemanship to amuse a small circle of visitors to the stable. I had not, however, noticed the railway line running alongside the stable courtyard.

I was walking along his bare back, wriggling my toes in his lovely soft coat and thoroughly enjoying myself, when the first train Hornero had ever seen steamed past.

The driver could not believe his eyes when he saw a gringa strolling on a horse's back. He waved and shouted and hooted his horn enthusiastically and grew very excited. So did Hornero, who made off with a series of enormous bucks. I flew to the ground, hit my side on something very hard and heard a loud crack.

Chapter Ten

When I opened my eyes again, Hornero was standing over me looking astonished at this new trick. I was in agony. Erwin dashed over. He felt my ribs and declared that some of them were broken. Then he bound me up with horse bandages and took me off to his home, to be looked after by his family.

That night I woke up in a panic. I had been put in the family's main bedroom. In the next bed Sara, Erwin's wife, snored gently in her sleep, and little two-year-old Gordito, dozing in her arms, was singing to himself. I dared not move for fear of disturbing them – and anyway I couldn't. I felt mad with frustration and fury at my own stupidity. I was trapped, shut in. I felt I was in prison, and it was true, I was.

I had been spoilt by freedom. The sunlight and the shadows of each very different day. Perfect independence. The endless adventure of the open road. Now I quickly discovered that I could not sit up by myself. I could not turn over. I could not even sneeze without my side giving an excruciating 'click, click, click'. Worst of all I was desperate for a wee . . .

Eventually I managed to lower my arm to the floor to touch what felt like the edge of a china chamber pot which Sara must have placed discreetly beside the bed. I almost knocked it over trying to get to it, and Sara awoke and helped me. My gratitude was mixed with acute embarrassment, a feeling that would become familiar over the next few days.

The following day they took me for an X-ray. It showed two ribs badly crushed, crossed like flat swords just missing my right lung. They would never be the same again, the doctor said. But where they crossed would become filled in with cementation and eventually they would be stronger than before. 'Only when the archaeologists find your skeleton in a thousand years' time there will be something unusual about it.' He smiled. 'Two months' complete rest are required.'

I just did not believe it. It seemed like a life sentence. The whole expedition was doomed. But surely I had heard of jockeys who had managed to ride in races with broken ribs?

Erwin and Sara persuaded the doctor that I should remain at their home instead of staying in hospital, and Erwin bought some local 'pipeno' wine to cheer me up. He nursed me as though I had four legs instead of two, binding me up with fresh bandages when I needed them.

How I wished, as I wrote to tell my publishers what had happened, that I was able to tell them that I had broken the ribs while falling down a mountain, or trying to leap a ravine – instead of having to confess that I had simply fallen off my horse while doing tricks, showing off in a stableyard. Needless to say, the only time I have ever fallen overboard at sea was during a flat calm . . .

Mine were not the only problems. The day after my accident, twenty-five carabineros' cars were blown up not far from Chiguayante. Four carabineros had been killed, and several more injured, as well as many civilians. Sorrow hung over the whole stable, especially Erwin's house. It was not the first such occurrence. A left-wing terrorist gang called the Manuel Rodríguez Group planted bombs with a frequency that made the IRA seem tame by comparison. In the wake of the latest incident the government had imposed a curfew in the area. Nobody was allowed to travel after 10 p.m. If they did have to drive somewhere in an emergency, they had to keep their lights on. Otherwise they risked getting shot at.

104

On 9 November Erwin brought Hornero and Jolgorio round to the front of the house where I could see them from the bedroom window. They looked very fit. The people at the stable, especially Erwin, had looked after them lovingly, even finding time to lunge them every day so that they would not lose condition.

Hornero had apparently not taken very kindly to being run in circles on a line, but it had certainly made all the difference to his fitness. I was more determined than ever to get on with the expedition as soon as possible. In the meantime I had to be content with the minor triumph of being able to stagger for the first time through the garden to the outside loo, escorted by a curious convoy of ducks, geese and hens.

Sara imposed her own magnificent presence on the strange little wooden house by the railway line. The cleanliness of the tiny kitchen may have been its only luxury, but I never had tasted such delicious meals. The back yard may have been a bit muddy and full of hens and ducks, but these inhabitants laid a generous supply of eggs in odd corners, and the crisp white sheets usually billowing above them from the washing lines were fit for a bed in a palace.

Sara was extraordinarily kind – and not just to me. I had already been struck by how the Chilean people survived, often in conditions of hardship, by showing a special compassion towards each other. Every day Sara would pass lunch over the fence to the unemployed cobbler who lived next door. He lived in a house much inferior to the stables the horses occupied at the equestrian school, but seemed quite content. He had no money, Sara said, but he sang to her and did her shopping – thus earning his lunch and his nickname of 'Luis the purse'. In the garden of his house grew beans and potatoes in wild profusion, and by the water pump in front of his hut beautiful roses which he sometimes managed to sell.

To Sara's vociferous disapproval, I decided to move back into my tent after a week. It was time, I thought, to begin clutching at the remnants of my independence. Even so Sara still insisted on coming every day, bringing me a picnic – so I was probably causing her more work even than before. She would arrive, effervescent with energy, and immediately busy herself sorting me out. She would pounce happily on my untidiness and other signs that I could not yet really manage, and bear my dirty laundry off like a trophy.

'*Toda la comida . . . toda la comida*. All the food,' she would insist, becoming quite angry if I did not eat everything she had brought. '*Tú estás muy flaca* . . . You are very thin.'

I loved her and Erwin, but sometimes she would drive me mad with her fussing. She almost assaulted me with kindness. And of course I knew I would never be able to repay it.

Erwin had erected the tent for me in a huge barn, on top of a deep cushion of soft hay. Even so, the simplest of tasks was a major undertaking. I had to think carefully about every movement beforehand, because bending forwards or sideways was still quite impossible and the ribs still kept clicking.

My first few days back in the tent would, I think, have made a good black comedy. Supporting parts were played by Rasca, the little brown-and-white terrier who was the stable's mascot, and Celis, the black stable cat, who both decided that the tent was their home too. One slept on one side of my sleeping-bag, the other on the other side. If either strayed into the other's territory I would have to duck down into the sleeping-bag while a flailing, spitting, scratching skirmish went on over my head. Luckily these never seemed to last for long, the dog usually giving up first. Then Rasca came on heat and there was even more chaos. She would arrive suddenly in the middle of the night seeking sanctuary, pursued by six or more enormous love-stricken dogs.

Two weeks passed. Gradually I became a little stronger, though I was now as afraid to look at the calendar as a spendthrift at his purse. Cape Horn's gentler summer face would not wait. The only way not to lose the time totally, I decided, was to try to use it for something else. I would get on with my writing.

106

The staff at the stable really entered into the spirit of helping me. No executive had a larger or more magnificent office than my barn after they had converted it into a giant writer's den. The grooms even constructed me a special desk out of jump poles and pieces of wood. And for my seat I had bags of the finest oats placed specially so as to give support to my ribs.

On 22 November I at last managed to clamber on board Hornero again and to trot feebly around the jumping enclosure. It was agony and I still had no strength at all in my right side or arm. The next day I tried again – and the next. Gradually riding became easier. When I wasn't practising on the horses, I tried to prepare for the next stage of the journey. The trips to Concepcíon on the swaying, bouncing bus were almost as painful as my sessions with Hornero.

Concepcíon was an elegant and well-ordered city. It seemed incredible that it had four times been almost completely destroyed by earthquakes or tidal waves – in 1570, 1640, 1653 and 1835. Its people were resilient: the early settlers had fought off attacks by pirates like Drake and Hawkins, and by the fierce Araucanian Indians, the original inhabitants of the area, under their great leader Caupolicán.

On 4 March 1835 Charles Darwin sailed into Concepcíon harbour in HMS *Beagle*, just ten days after a terrible earthquake had devastated the city. Darwin wrote about the experience of Mr Rouse, then British Consul in Concepcíon:

' . . . The first movement warned him to run out. He had scarcely reached the middle of the courtyard when one side of his house came thundering down. He retained the presence of mind to remember that if he once got on the top of that part which had already fallen, he would be safe . . . but he had no sooner ascended this, than the other side of the house fell in, the great beams sweeping close in front of his head. With his eyes blinded and his mouth choked with the cloud of dust which darkened the sky, he at last gained the street.

107

' . . . As shock succeeded shock at the interval of a few minutes, no one dared approach the remains of the buildings . . . Hundreds knew themselves ruined and few had the means of providing food for the day . . . '

Darwin suggested that if the earth's crust were to be as unstable in England as it was in Chile, the country would be bankrupt and in chaos: 'In every large town famine would go forth, pestilence and death following in its train . . . ' Yet somehow Concepcíon had survived.

The city had originally been founded by the same Captain Pedro de Valdivia who had taken possession of Santiago valley and many other towns and cities in Chile. He had had, it seemed, a most interesting lady companion called Inés de Suárez. Once, while he was away from a settlement, it was attacked by Indians. Inés killed the Indian hostages the attackers were trying to rescue, chopping their heads off herself with a hatchet and flinging them at the attackers, who fled in consternation. When Pedro was eventually captured by Indians, they got their revenge by eating him alive . . . slowly!

On 6 December, a month later than I originally intended, we left Chiguayante. We headed south, to Coronel then on to Lota, Carampangue, Ramadillas . . . The ribs had still not closed properly and were painful. They were still swathed in horsebandages which shrank and nearly squeezed me to death every time it rained. When this happened I would have to stop immediately, make for the nearest bushes and then entertain the horses to a strange-looking striptease, unwinding everything and then starting all over again!

Although frisky after their long rest, the horses seemed to understand that I needed gentle treatment. Once or twice, however, their high spirits got the better of them and, as I had no strength to hold them, we would set off on a mad gallop which would last for miles, until all their excess energy had been used up. Then we would have to plod back, so that I could pick up all the things which had fallen off the packsaddle.

Ironically, our route for the first two days took us parallel to the railway line. I spent most of the first day getting off every time I heard a train coming, tying the horses firmly to a tree to wait till it had passed. Saddling up was still very difficult, loads having to be levered up with the help of my knee. Tightening the girths enough was another problem. Everything had to be done very, very slowly.

It was a great credit to Jolgorio's patience that I managed. His reward was that there seemed to be as many trees in this part of Chile as there was sand in the desert – and now nobody minded if he nibbled at one or two – or even at a great many.

LOG: *7 December 1984*
We are now right in the middle of the coal-mining district of Chile, which like that of Wales is mountainous and very beautiful. Conditions, however, are very hard for the miners. It does not, it seems, need the involvement of either an Arthur Scargill or a Coal Board for there to be unrest in mining areas. Unemployment and pit closures are, I learnt, worldwide problems. Here the people do not smile so much, and little boys are apt to throw stones. Also I have been told there are bandits – though thank God, I have not met any personally yet . . . To be on the safe side, we go more or less into hiding every night. Either among the trees or behind a rock – or near a house, if we can find one. The tent is holding up as well against the constant rainstorms as it did the sandstorms northward. Also the camera and tape-recorder have so far survived well in the new plastic boxes I bought in Concepcíon as insurance premiums against damp.

Where shall I be for Christmas? I don't know. Probably with the horses on the top of some mountain, with Hornero and Jolgorio wearing flowers in their bridles for the occasion!

I am thinking of asking the local people to show me how to snare rabbits and other game, because I believe that food may be a problem for me from Puerto Montt southward.

8 December was a holiday in Chile. We camped in a park in Curanilahue, where some miners invited me to a picnic consisting mostly of some very strong punch which made me forget about my ribs. One of them gave me a beautiful red blanket for the horses. From there we travelled slowly southward via Cañete, Lago Lleulleu, Quidico . . . Gradually the appearance of the homesteads and houses was changing, the doorways and the rooms becoming smaller to match the size of the people. I began to feel like Gulliver in Lilliput.

I was now out of the coal-mining area and in the heart of the Mapuche and Araucanian Indian country. The people, once brave and famous warriors, and as big a scourge to the early settlers as the earthquakes themselves, are now very kindly and hospitable to strangers.

My small and painstakingly acquired vocabulary of Spanish was not much appreciated here. Instead the Mapuches tried to teach me a few words of their own Indian dialect. Here bread was not *pan* but *cobque*; water not *agua* but *co*; and a horse, or *caballo*, was a *cahuello*.

I rode along a deserted cliffside road towards Tirua. Looking back down each steep hill we had climbed at the tight zigzags cutting the green of the countryside behind us, I felt that nowhere in the world could there possibly be more road per kilometre of crow-flying distance. When we eventually reached Tirua the yellow track elbowed itself dramatically down to sea level before zigzagging up yet another hill. An old woman laughed as I desperately clung on to my sombrero. 'Here,' she said in heavily accented Spanish, '*el viento malo*, the bad wind, never stops.' In spite of the lush vegetation of the area Tirua reminded me of some of the desert towns. The little settlement seemed very isolated, and gave the impression that it had not grown up naturally, but had been brought here piece by piece. The people mostly lived in shiny rows of brand new subsidized houses, erected by the government in order to tempt them south from the shanty town areas of Santiago and other crowded cities. For here the teeming sea provided an especially thriving fishing industry, creating work. There was a smart little police station and a brand new medical post.

It had been a hard ride. I went to this little hospital so that the nurse could have a look at my ribs, and disgraced myself by falling asleep on the waiting-room bench.

To seaward of Tirua was the island of Mocha, where in 1571 Francis Drake had enjoyed a different form of Chilean welcome. Having gone ashore for water, he and his men had run into a band of about one hundred Indians, who had rained arrows on them. According to George Malcolm Thomson's account, every man of Drake's party had been hit, Drake himself being struck by three arrows. He had not been hurt seriously enough to prevent him sailing northward on the next fair wind, to Valparaíso, at that time a little village of no more than nine houses. He had pillaged it ruthlessly, even taking the altar cloth from the chapel. His efforts had not stopped there. Lying off Valparaiso was the Spanish ship *Grand Captain of the South*. This Drake had also taken, together with her treasure of 25,000 pesos of gold and a large crucifix set with emeralds.

Next day on the same dusty track, with the sea on one side and the mountains on the other, I encountered some very cheerful-looking evangelists singing hymns on horseback. They swooped down upon the horses and myself and escorted us back to their house, which was built close to a beautiful waterfall cascading down from the mountains. They invited me in for supper and more hymns sung to the accompaniment of guitar and tambourine, and I struggled to

111

record as much as possible on my little recorder.

When night fell, they took my horses by their halters and me by the arm and led us firmly to the little wooden church beside the house. They ushered us all inside. Tying Hornero and Jolgorio to the ends of the pews and throwing down armfuls of hay, they insisted, 'You shall all sleep here. It will be more sheltered from the rain.'

When I protested I was told that 'Jesús El Señor was born in a stable – was he not?' It was a charming thought, but I nevertheless covered the floor with some old sacking I found outside, especially the area under Hornero's and Jolgorio's rear ends!

Chapter Eleven

On the outskirts of Trovolhue we met a woman on her way to town to do her shopping. She was a friendly plump lady. In England you could imagine her driving the family car to the supermarket. Instead she was mounted on a magnificent bay stallion with her three little daughters perched behind.

The little girls were having trouble with their shoes, which were too big and kept falling off. So, in spite of Hornero's annoyance, we trotted behind and rescued the shoes each time they fell. The children laughed in delight each time I handed them back, but Mamma and the stallion took little notice.

Trovolhue lay inland, the centre of a closely cupped hand of dark green mountains. It seemed like some frontier town of a hundred years ago. 'The Wild West is alive and well,' I thought, as I rode in. 'It is just that it has moved down south a bit.'

Horses were hitched up in rows outside the village bar, the shops, the police station, even outside the little church. The few people I saw on foot seemed an entirely different inferior species to those mounted. A man might be old, bent or bald, but once on his horse he underwent a transformation and assumed magnificence.

Apart from horses, the only traffic in Trovolhue was the huge lumbering carts drawn by splendid pairs of oxen. Some of these beasts, probably because of their enormous weight and the consequent pressure on their feet, were shod in specially designed iron shoes to fit their cloven hooves.

We camped for the night in a lush damp field owned by an old man who told me his great grandfather had been a pianomaker in Hamburg. His prize piano, which he had brought with him all the way from Germany, had been shipwrecked with him off Puerto Saavedra, while he had been searching for a place to settle in 1851. Both had been rescued and the instrument was apparently still tuneful enough for the pianomaker to demonstrate its playing to such effect that he had been able to start the first piano manufacturing business in Chile.

His great grandfather had eventually died aged ninety-eight, but the old piano lived on. It stood on three legs in a corner of the old man's living-room. We stared at it in silent reverence.

'Whether it can still play is this piano's own secret,' my host said at last. 'Since Great Grandfather died nobody has been allowed to touch it.'

Next day we moved on, creeping through the mountains' fingers, past a splendid forest of monkey puzzle trees which looked as though they had been stolen from a hundred suburban gardens in England – instead of vice versa.

From here we passed into a fertile-looking valley, riding along the banks of Río Imperial on a beautiful path lined with willow trees. Rivers always hold a lure for me, so we stopped a day at the pretty village of Carahue which lay just before the bridge across the Imperial, and I was able to engage in such mundane but essential chores as mending bits of saddlery and doing my washing. The following morning we left early, crossing the bridge.

It was clear that in this area nobody thought my journeying with two horses strange. Men working in the fields would raise their hats as I passed by and politely ask, '*Pasando?* Are you travelling?'

The only thing they did find extraordinary was my pack-saddle. No one used them in this part of Chile, it seemed, preferring instead to have just one horse and to gallop at full speed to the next town or hostelry. Distances were measured not in kilometres, but in how many hours it would take to get there on horseback – an estimate that, because of the packs, I had to double.

The sun was just setting as we reached the causeway across the inlet to Lake Budi, the largest saltwater lake in South America. It was the end of market day at the little town of Puerto Domínguez which stands on the edge of the lake; oxen carts jammed as tightly as the traffic at Marble Arch were silhouetted against the water. The water seemed like an orange extension of the sky, its little waves edged with gold. I felt I had arrived, not just at another Chilean town, but in another age.

As I approached the centre of the town three little girls rushed up and, grabbing my horses' reins, led us off to meet their father. I was invited to put Hornero and Jolgorio in his stable with a good feed of oats, and to stay for what he said would be a very special supper.

The main ingredient of the meal walked into the kitchen shortly afterwards, on its own four legs, and promptly stole a piece of cabbage off the kitchen table. The young man who was leading the sheep petted and stroked it as he tied it up. Then he gently pared the wool away from its neck, near the jugular vein. Someone handed him a bottle and he poured a generous slug of what looked like the local cognac down the sheep's throat and then another down his own. Then he got out his knife again.

The sheep seemed quite unafraid, even content, especially after the drink. I could hardly bear to look. One quick cut and it was all over. The family's little maid rushed up and poured a bowl of spicy liquid into the gash. It was important, my host explained, to do this before the reflexes stopped twitching, so that the spices could circulate in the blood and flavour the meat. Ugh! I thought. But the youngest child never even paused as she did a drawing in my log book. She and the other

115

girls had viewed the whole proceedings with an indifference that was perhaps no more than total lack of hypocrisy. In the countryside of southern Chile, legs of mutton are not found in neat rows of twenty, lining supermarket shelves.

It was now just 250 kilometres, or one week's fast riding, to Pargua. There I would cross the narrow channel of Chacao to the island of Chiloé, then cross the Gulf of Ancud from the port of Chonchi to Chaitén and on to the far southern archipelago of South America, large parts of which are still totally unexplored.

The immediate next stage of my journey was through the Lake District, described by the guidebooks as the most beautiful part of Chile. To landward of me lay Villarrica, Pucón, Pullinque, Lago Riñihue, a glorious backpacker's heaven, endowed with dozens of spectacular snowcapped volcanoes and lakes and rapidly becoming established as the thriving heart of Chile's tourist industry. There were dozens of places I could happily have spent months or even years exploring. But I dared not deviate from my route. The shadow of the Horn still hung over my every move. If I could not keep up the discipline of travelling south towards the wilderness, harbouring my slender resources of will, time and money, then I would never get there. I would never get back to Cape Horn at all.

The whole adventure had been planned to last four months. It had looked possible at the start, walking down the map with my dividers, nearly marking off fifty kilometres a day. However, I had already been travelling for five months, and the difficult part of the expedition was really only just beginning. Also, in spite of my simple lifestyle, my funds would not last forever. I had been overwhelmed by the hospitality and kindness shown me all the way down Chile, but it would have been morally wrong as well as humiliating to have depended on it.

So I had to steel myself and hurry through paradise. For once the secret of good progress seemed to be not to study the

116

map of the area too closely and risk becoming beguiled by wonderful-sounding places. 'I can always go back one day,' I said to myself, not quite believing it, as I headed determinedly southwards, clinging to the coast with its little farms, away from the tentacles of tourism.

We passed Hualpin, where Jolgorio ran off ten miles in the wrong direction after I had become distracted trying to take a photograph and he had somehow got the lead rope caught under his tail. After he had been safely retrieved, I rode to the edge of the swollen River Toltén, where the horses had to board the first rickety river raft they had ever seen.

At this stage they were still quite afraid of the water and only this kept them from leaping overboard, packs and all, as the ramshackle craft shuddered and creaked on its way, propelled only by the fierce current and the willpower of an old boatman with a broken paddle.

The following evening we arrive in Nueva, or 'New', Toltén. The first part of its name had been very hard won, and if the little town looked like a Dutch village it was no accident.

In 1960 Toltén was totally destroyed by the same earthquake and tidal wave which had badly damaged most of the main buildings in the nearby city of Valdivia. A lady of Scottish descent, who had married a Chilean and lived in Toltén for fifty-three years, showed me pictures of the old town with the very tops of the roofs of the houses looking like the half-submerged hulls of a flotilla of upturned boats.

The people of the Netherlands had been especially sympathetic, perhaps because of their own perpetual battle to keep out the sea. They had raised a fund and had sent over experts to build sea defences and architects to build new houses. Now Nueva Toltén was a neat town which could easily have been in the Netherlands, and no scars remained except in the inhabitants' memories.

We climbed a hilly coast road through Queule, then passed through the suburbs of Valdivia with their lush avenues of

117

apple-trees heavily laden with unripe apples. The trees were no doubt direct descendants of those described by Darwin on his visit to Valdivia in 1835.

South of Valdivia towards La Unión and Río Bueno, I noticed a change. I no longer had to duck through the doorways of the houses and the people were taller and blonder – more like myself. The beautifully kept farms and picturesque wooden farmhouses could have been in Germany. Indeed many of the farmers greeted me in German as I passed, perhaps mistaking me for one of themselves.

In 1850 a law was passed which permitted up to 2500 German nationals to settle in the south of Chile. These were later followed by others, mostly from Bavaria. Facilities such as long-term interest-free loans and cheap land were made available to these *chilenos alemanes*, as the other Chileans referred to them, in return for their considerable farming skills and hard work, all of which helped to develop that part of Chile lying between Valdivia and Puerto Montt.

Just in time for Christmas we arrived at Osorno and the sanctuary of Comandante René Varas' famous showjumping stables. Once again my horses were a passport to an experience that would surely have been denied me had I been travelling by any other means.

René Varas and his famous horse Quintral had won a gold medal in the Munich Olympics in 1972. This achievement was all the more remarkable because René and his team had undergone the ordeal of a stormy three-week voyage from Chile beforehand, during which time the horses had been able to get no exercise.

'I have been waiting for you for twelve years,' he said as he greeted me. 'Anything I can do for your horses will be a small repayment for the moral obligation I owe one Inspector Smith of the Royal Society for the Prevention of Cruelty to Animals in Liverpool.'

René explained that after the Olympics and other international competitions in Europe, he had been stranded in

Liverpool. The ship that was to take him and his team back to Chile had been delayed by storms and he had been very worried about his horses, having managed to buy only enough corn and fodder for the long voyage itself. Inspector Smith had come to the rescue and had looked after the team until the ship had finally arrived, twenty-five days overdue. René had never forgotten it.

He introduced me to the magnificent Quintral, now very old but living happily in the stable's most luxurious loosebox together with his pet goat. Then I was invited to a Christmas Eve 'concourse' or competition for René's team of young riders. All the *huaso*'s pride and talent, all his subtle, disciplined horsemanship was still there, blended with the English style of showjumping; the result was remarkable to watch. I wished I had a movie camera so that I could have recorded the Chileans' performance for people to see back home. Or better still, that a Chilean team might in the near future visit England and Europe again. René shook his head sadly when I suggested this. 'That is the dream of every young rider here,' he said. 'But nowadays travelling is so expensive and we are so very far away.' He explained that there was also great difficulty in finding horses here with Olympic or international potential. Cost and distance prohibited most Chilean breeders from having access to the best thoroughbred stallions, these being based mostly overseas. Quintral had been one in ten thousand.

Later I sat in the Varas family's living-room, touched by the fact that there were presents under the Christmas tree for me as well, including a lovely silver salver. The opening of these was presided over by René's sixteen-year-old daughter Marcela as the clock struck midnight and Christmas Day began. It meant a great deal to be in the midst of a family. I kept thinking about my own children, worried that they might be missing me – and equally worried that they might not be!

The Varases' house was quite different from the quaint

119

wooden houses which seemed so typical of this part of Chile. From the outside it looked like an ordinary stone bungalow of the kind you might find anywhere in the world. But inside it was quite unique, a shrine to René's horses, especially to his beloved Quintral. An almost lifesize photo of the great horse covered the wall of the passage to the bathroom and in front of it were other photos, cups, tankards, medals, trophies, rosettes, won by René in many parts of the world.

I spent Christmas Day morning lying in the soft grass of the jumping stadium in my bikini, watching my horses grazing happily among the jumps. Three days later I set off again, feeling naked as I had arranged to have my packs sent on to Pargua. It was the last chance to rest Jolgorio's back before the wilderness. René had arranged for me to stay with friends of his all along the way, but I still felt extraordinarily helpless and homeless, being without my tent for the first time on the journey. I began suffering from an epidemic of small accidents. Between Christmas and New Year I managed to break my thumb, the ribs started hurting again, and I tore my hand open. Apart from this all went well, and Jolgorio's back benefited greatly from the extra rest.

In Puerto Octay Hornero had an accident: he made off with a bride, flowing white gown and all! We had met the bridal party by the shores of Lake Llanquihue and she had been perched on Hornero's back for a photograph. He had become alarmed by her white veil and galloped away with her hanging on for dear life. Luckily it turned out she was a good horsewoman and her anxious new husband retrieved her unhurt. I rode on towards Quilanto happily munching several sturdy slices of wedding cake. There I was met once again by mounted carabineros who accompanied me at a mad gallop which almost turned into a race, into the beautiful German town of Frutillar. 'Señor Leslie is waiting for you,' they said mysteriously.

Frutillar looked a town too good to be touched without gloves, a place where mud had never been invented. On one

120

side of the main road velvety grass and flower gardens merged gently with the deep evening blue of Lake Lanquihue while the top of Osorno Volcano loomed over the other side; it seemed to be floating on air, for all I could see was the white crater. On the volcano side of the road were a museum, neat wooden houses mostly painted bright blue and a beautiful yellow shingled church with a strange hexagonal steeple.

Señor Leslie, whose farm was just beyond the village, turned out to be 'Lucky' Edwin Leslie, whose ancestors came from Scotland. His father and grandfather had been born in Buenos Aires, the grandfather being Norman Leslie, OBE, British Vice-Consul in Montevideo during the Battle of the River Plate.

Edwin was very Scottish at heart, proud that the Leslie clan still had its own tartan and its motto 'Gripfast'. He and his English wife Jane made me and the horses very welcome. They had been trying to get in touch with me via the Claro Liras ever since I had left the hacienda.

Jane lent me one of her best party dresses, in which I felt quite awkward, having worn nothing but tracksuits for so long, and they took me off to a German-style New Year's Eve party at Frutillar's Gimnasio del Instituto.

The German instinct for organized pageantry and sentiment mixed with Chilean enthusiasm made a powerful cocktail and made me feel rather nostalgic. After dinner the young people got up to dance, while their parents, who seemed to be the cream of Frutillar society, mingled and chatted and politely wished me well.

I thought back to the little baby 'Rosie'; to the woman with green eyes; to the splendour of the hacienda; to Erwin the vet and Sara and to all the other homes in Chile where I had been made so welcome, never arriving as anything else than a total stranger, yet never receiving anything but greatest kindness – and I wondered what they were all doing now. Most of all I wondered what was happening at home in Wales.

121

At last twelve o'clock struck and voices filled the hall with a German version of 'Auld Lang Syne'. There was no one I wanted to kiss. So instead I raised my glass in a toast to my children and those I loved twelve thousand miles away. Also to gallant Hornero and Jolgorio busy eating thistles in one of Edwin's fields – and to the fabulous year that had passed. 1984, the year of George Orwell and the year of the horse!

When I said goodbye to the Leslies on 2 January I was wearing Edwin's Patagonian walking boots, which he had had ever since he'd been a young sheep farmer down in Tierra del Fuego. They were much too big and I kept tripping over the toes, but wearing them made me somehow feel closer to Patagonia myself.

I rode all morning along the lakeside, past the village of Llanquihue itself. Arriving in Puerto Varas that afternoon, I thought I recognized the Range Rover coming towards me. I certainly recognized the faces – it was John and Jenny Hickman coming to meet me for the second time on this adventure, a delightful surprise. Over tea they explained they were on holiday with their family in Puyehue near Osorno and had to get back before evening. Having heard disturbing rumours about my breaking my ribs, they thought they had better drive down to see how I really was. Their thoughtfulness gave me a glow which immediately cured the last vestiges of the aches in my bones.

I spent the night in a large green wooden house, overlooking the lake. The moon rose just above the snowy crater of the volcano, looking indescribably beautiful. The old couple who had offered me hospitality must have been well over eighty, but all through the evening they kept holding hands. Well, if ever there was a place on earth where one could feel young and romantic forever, this was it.

Two days later found me lying on the warm and windy sand of Pargua, the Land's End of the main body of Chile. It was very peaceful. The only creatures on the beach were some seals and a very fat old woman, buried deep in the sand

122

to cure her lumbago. I had to undig her to borrow a pen.

It was an unlikely venue for deep thought. But I knew I was at the last crossroads of the journey. This was the brink of the wilderness. Whatever decision I made I would have to stick to, there would be no going back.

The day before, I had visited Puerto Montt, the quaint Nordic-style fishing port which looks out over Reloncaví Sound and is the southern terminal of both the road and railway in Chile. There I had struggled hard to exchange questions for answers.

The easiest route down the archipelago to Tierra del Fuego would be through the pampas of Argentina, or at least having access to the gentler terrain of that country whenever the going on the Chilean side became impossible. But the Falklands War still overshadowed relations between Britain and Argentina and I was not sure the Argentinians would let me in. British businessmen had apparently been able to enter Argentina since shortly after the war, but it was still, I was told, virtually impossible for me to get an ordinary tourist visa to go there. There was, however, an even greater obstacle. The Chilean Agricultural Society informed me that because there was swine fever in Argentina and not in Chile, Hornero and Jolgorio would be subject to forty days' quarantine every time they crossed the border and there might be a risk of not being allowed back into Chile at all. So, Argentina, so tantalizingly close, could not be part of this expedition. It made everything much harder.

I had two choices. I could take a ferry from Puerto Montt to Punta Arenas. The journey through the channels, islands and fjords of the southern archipelago takes about five days and for centuries was the only Chilean link between the two ports. That way I could still get to Cape Horn in summer when it was much easier to land there – and keep all my promises. Alternatively, we could still try to go most of the way by land. A recently blasted, partly completed track would ease the first part, but for hundreds of kilometres we

123

would have to fight our way through a part of the world totally unchanged by man since time began. The archipelago of Chile is the stormiest, rainiest place on earth. It has swamps, impenetrable jungle, icecaps and fjords. It has tortuous mazes of uninhabited islands which are the tops of enormous underwater mountains. In the *South American Handbook* it is described as 'veritable topographical hysteria'.

This journey could take more than five months and there was a chance that we might not arrive at the other end. Should I take the easier way and be sure of reaching my destination? I remembered writing, 'An adventure is not merely geographical.' If I went by ferry, the expedition would no longer be as I had imagined it. Somehow, I was still convinced that the reward of seeing Cape Horn again would be measured in terms of the pain of getting there. If I went by ferry, I might reach my goal but miss it at the same time.

As dusk fell and I made my way to my campsite, having been reunited with my tent again in Pargua, I realized that there had not been a decision to make after all. The lure of the archipelago was far too strong; the chance to explore it would never come again. People said it was an 'impossible' part of the world, but as I had once optimistically written, 'impossible' usually means only 'nearly impossible' – and the 'nearly' is the adventure.

A place guarded so fiercely by nature had to be very special, the home of creatures and plants not found anywhere else in the world in the wild: black-necked swans, trees which are over five thousand years old, pumas, silver foxes, albatross; the breeding ground of condors, mysteries and rare dreams. My mind was made up.

Next day the horses and I crossed the Canal de Chacao to the island of Chiloé, famous for its churches, its seafaring history and its adventurous people. The horses and I viewed most of Chiloé through the leafy branches stuck in my hat and their bridles in an attempt to try and discourage the enormous orange-coloured flies which pursued us relentlessly. The secret seemed to be to break into a full gallop every now and again. We would leave our unwanted entourage behind for a while, but they soon caught up again.

On 10 January, our first night on the island, we reached Ancud, where they make the famous *chalupa* clinch-built fishing-boats, which are superbly adapted to the treacherous South Pacific. Though open and powered only by oars, or when the wind is favourable by rough sails sewn out of flour sacks, they still carry the Chilotes on sea-fishing expeditions which sometimes last for weeks.

From Ancud we travelled south through beautiful sunshine. Except for the unique daintily-built and brightly-coloured churches and little wooden houses, the countryside looked a bit like the wilder parts of England. Ambling through giant daisies and dandelions and lush purple clover, Hornero and Jolgorio seemed to be becoming fatter every hour. One horseman I met said that he thought my horses much too fat. I didn't agree. Our food supply was never secure. We had been through the Atacama. Now there was the archipelago ahead. Times might become hard again. Camels may have humps, but poor Hornero and Jolgorio had to keep their food reserves somewhere else!

On the way to Castro I felt quite ill with a bad stomach ache. Every bump hurt. So instead of riding I stumbled along the dusty road on foot, the horses following patiently behind. After walking several kilometres I came to a strange-looking house, built on stilts so far out into a small lake that it seemed as though the stilts themselves had wandered absent-mindedly out into the water and forgotten how to turn back.

As I got closer, the sounds of merry singing, rather than any written sign, proclaimed it to be one of those bars without set opening hours but with plenty of life and – if my experiences in the rest of Chile were any guide – a warm welcome for the travelling stranger. I managed to clamber up the steps to a little veranda leading to the door and went in.

The welcome was as I expected even though the patrons were plainly surprised to see someone staggering *into* a bar. They were all Chilote Indians. Several chairs were produced all at once for me to sit down in and a friendly-looking woman tucked a beautiful rug of Chilote homespun wool around me. Most of the people there were elderly except for a little boy, who could not have been more than eight but seemed to be in charge of the bar. He handed me a glass, telling me, 'The fire will burn your pain . . . '

He was right. I soon felt well enough to listen to the old men's stories, straining my still elementary Spanish to understand their particular accent. Nearly all these Chilote Indians had brothers or cousins or friends who had left the family home, sometimes as young as ten years old, in order to go and search for adventure and a new life in the wilderness of the archipelago. No, they had not come back. They had not seen them for twenty, thirty, fifty years . . . But yes, they thought they were still there.

I thought of the guidebooks I had read stating, 'Between Puerto Montt and Punta Arenas there is nothing . . . ' But there was! Long, long before anyone else in Chile or in the world had dared to think of it, the Chilotes had set off in their little open boats to brave the southern archipelago. The pioneering spirit of these people was an inspiration.

Early next morning, feeling totally recovered after a good rest, I set off again – this time persecuted by mosquitoes. Maybe they liked the alcohol in my blood!

On 12 January I rode into the picturesque capital of Chiloé, Castro, where the horses, with typical Chilote hospitality, were let loose in the rose garden of the local chief of police. I prayed that they would concentrate on the clover in his lawn rather than on the roses.

For my dinner, I went to one of the numerous tumble-down waterfront restaurants again built on stilts as seemed to be the custom here and sticking out into the sea. Here they served strange multi-coloured local seafood for the equivalent of about twenty new pence and also white wine to wash it down with at about five pence a glass. I, too, was in clover.

A little later, passing stalls laden with a luxuriant array of woollen scarves, ponchos, jerseys and socks, I decided to exchange one of the last of my original batch of traveller's cheques for a poncho. I would need something to keep me warm during the bitter weather which I knew must lie ahead.

Next day I rode along the shore past a maze of inlets and islands to the little port of Chonchi, where I hoped to catch a ferry to Chaitén on the mainland. The town looked as though it had been poured over the hill, with a steep drop down to the dock area on one side and to the little stony beach on the other. I pitched my tent a little way along this shoreline, in the lee of some bent trees. Secluded, I thought, but not from all visitors – for that night I was visited by a troop of grey foxes, just visible in the moonlight, shyly peeping round my tent flap for a look, then hurrying away, only to scamper back again. This game lasted several hours, with me lying very still for fear of frightening them. 'Pigs, cats, dogs – and now foxes!' I thought. 'I really ought to start an animals' Visitor's Book.' It was one of the joys of living in a small green tent. Animals seemed to lose the fear they had of other human dwellings and came right up to – even into – the tent.

In the morning I took the horses paddling. Then I went to see about our tickets for the ferry crossing from Chonchi to Chaitén. I was astonished to find myself at the tail of a queue of the first real tourists I had seen in Chile. It was the last thing I expected at this stage. It seemed they were all going to Chaitén. Parts of the new road, the Carretera Austral, were opening up terrain where there never had been a track before and people from as far as Santiago were rushing here to explore a part of their country which previously had been inaccessible to them. Because of all the tourists in their cars, the ferry owners were most reluctant to take Hornero and

Jolgorio. I had to get special permission for the journey, and only after a great deal of pleading was I given a ticket for the following Thursday.

The night before we were due to sail a gale suddenly blew up just as I was getting into my sleeping-bag. The poor tent shook and twisted as though it was being tortured. I used up all the spare rope from the horses' headcollars as extra guy ropes and tried to build a wind-break with stones from the beach. The horses couldn't understand it at all. They ran wildly round and round their field. The wind had a power I had not felt for years. Next morning I studied the map. Yes! We were now at latitude 42 degrees and 40 minutes south. We had reached the Roaring Forties at last. Cape Horn was getting closer!

Chapter Twelve

As the ferry approached the mainland near Chaitén, I gazed overwhelmed at huge mountains covered for hundreds of miles by the fiercest, densest dark green forest that I had ever seen. It seemed incredible that in the same country at the start of my adventure I had ridden through nearly a thousand miles where there had not been even one tree or blade of grass. Contrast was too gentle a word for it. Chile was a country whose ingredients God had forgotten to stir.

The little town of Chaitén itself was a poignant pause amid the drama of the mountains, a monument to the pioneers of the turn of the century. Neat tin-roofed wooden houses clutched the mountainsides against the backdrop of the wilderness, the smell and the taste of the rain forest all around pervading every breath.

In this part of the country civilization and mobility were confined to a rough, partly finished road proudly called the Carretera Austral, blasted by determination and dynamite through virgin forest and stretching south towards Coihaique. I could hardly wait to set off along this mysterious road, and even more to explore the jungle on either side, to camp each night in a place where no human had ever slept before. After the delay waiting for the ferry from Chonchi to Chaitén and the lengthy negotiations to obtain passage for the horses, I felt free again. All I had to do was to buy a few provisions the next day, then saddle up Hornero and Jolgorio and go. But it was not to be.

129

At first all went well. The people of Chaitén were true pioneers. Hardship was always a handspan away, and the hospitality they showed me was almost ferocious. Within minutes of disembarking from the ferry a young woman called Naomi, granddaughter of the very first settler in Chaitén, almost literally dragged me off for a meal and a bath while the horses were offered yet another garden to eat. Naomi and her young friends all pinned pictures of themselves in my log book. 'So that you can send us some gringos from England!' they explained.

Later an old man, a horse nurse, arrived to admire my horses. After producing a card to show he had once worked at General Mendoza's jumping stable, he offered to change their shoes. Afterwards Hornero seemed ill at ease, but I put it down to nerves, caused by the fierce wind that blew incessantly from the mountains.

That night a great electric storm blew up and blazed across the tin roofs of the town; the torrents of rain seemed almost solid. Illumined by lightning the horses' tails fanned out against the wind and rain as they plunged around the garden neighing with fear. I managed to catch them and rubbed a little oil into their thin summer coats, a trick Dai Bowen had told me about for making horses' coats weatherproof. Having sacrificed the flysheet of my tent to make them raincoat ponchos, I let them loose again, thinking this might be safest and that moving about might at least prevent them from catching pneumonia. Then, calling out soothing promises and lies to them, I curled up in my tent, wondering why I had refused all the beds which had been offered me and trying to make myself feel warmer by conjuring up images of the searing Atacama sun or even of sunny Chiloé just a week before.

I woke in the middle of the night to find my sleeping-bag a saturated sponge and the tent gone. After staggering about blindly in the dark I eventually discovered it caught in some trees on the other side of the garden, a flash of lightning

130

revealing it as a giant Mary Poppins umbrella. It nearly carried me away as I struggled to retrieve it.

Having got the tent down from the trees, I tried to anchor it with my extra long and sharp iron tentpegs, but one of these boomeranged out and caught me just above the eye. It also tore a large hole in the tent. When dawn at last broke I was surrounded by indescribable chaos. The horses were still galloping around, from time to time stopping and backing into the storm, letting fly with their heels as though to frighten the sheets of rain away.

I retrieved my camera out of one pool of water, the tapes out of another. My small bag of flour had turned into paste. The tape-recorder was floating like a goldfish won at a fair in a plastic bag full of rainwater. When I'd mopped it dry I optimistically pressed the 'play' button. It emitted a dying croak. Everything I owned squelched, including me. Before I could set off I would have to get my equipment sorted out. It was no use all my new friends, who had offered me hospitality at their houses, saying, 'We told you so!' They would not be there to help me in the weeks ahead. I simply had to get used to living in a part of the world where it sometimes rains for 340 days a year.

But all the minor disasters of the night faded away when I examined the horses and discovered that Hornero was badly lame in his off fore hoof. The horse nurse said he must have been badly frightened by the storm and knocked himself while galloping about. In spite of the old man's kindly smiling face Hornero did not seem to like him: he laid his ears back flat as the man approached. What was needed, he said, was three days' rest and all would be fine. Sweat and rain poured down his face as he struggled to get the shoes he had put on the night before off again. 'That is nothing but a *burro*, a donkey,' he muttered, scowling at the nervous horse after he had finished.

His wife was more concerned about the cut above my eye. 'You must go to the hospital to have it stitched,' she said. But

I never got there. Before I reached the entrance of Chaitén's little hospital, a small boy ran up and, grabbing the edge of my poncho, pulled me into a side street.

'Come this way, this way,' he insisted. 'The witch lady Mimi wishes to see you.' It was an invitation I couldn't resist.

Mimi looked like a character from Noel Coward's *Blithe Spirit*, with pale gold hair wafting around an ageless face. Her living-room was crammed with gifts from her grateful patients. Bunches of leaves stuck out from behind the family portraits. Locks of hair were draped over china dogs and cats. Children's drawings crowded the mantlepiece.

'My patients often cannot afford to pay,' she whispered, 'but always they like to give something. I prescribe herbs and a few kind words and they feel better. Some people here in Chaitén call me a witch, but sometimes magic is very practical. Your case is an example.' She led me into her modern-looking kitchen and, opening the freezer, got out three raw steaks.

'Put these over the cut,' she instructed, 'and it will never swell up, no stitches will be needed and no scar show.'

I went to sleep that afternoon with the steaks over my eye and awoke to a growl coming from the corner of my tent. The horse nurse's dog was sitting there, slavering. After a few minutes I gave up the battle of wills and tossed the meat to him. Mimi's magic worked: the eye never did swell up and next morning I felt much better. Not so poor Hornero, who was evidently in considerable pain. Few horse medicines were available in Chaitén so over the next few days I made deep inroads into my own veterinary supplies, giving the horse fenilbutazona disinflammatory and pain-killing injections. Days passed and still his hoof remained hot to the touch. In spite of the rest he seemed to be becoming worse instead of better.

The horse nurse still insisted that all the evidence pointed to Hornero having hurt himself during the storm. The local blacksmith suggested the trouble might be permanent tendonitis caused by walking too many thousands of kilometres on the journey. A vet, passing through the town on holiday, pronounced the most gloomy diagnosis of all. 'I think he's broken a small bone in his foot,' he said. 'What a pity you can't get an X-ray.' Whichever diagnosis was correct, it was clear that Hornero was in great pain, hanging his neck for the first time on the journey. Jolgorio stayed by his friend's side, from time to time nudging him sympathetically.

I was in complete despair. I felt helpless and ashamed. I remember the difficulty I had had coping with the horses in the Atacama: how they had kept trying to run away; how I had lost them in the sandstorm; their suspicion of me, their mistrust. Now, having painstakingly taught them to trust me, I could do nothing to help them. Hornero whinnied anxiously every time I went out of sight, and the look of hope in his expressive brown eyes whenever I reappeared twisted my heart. If only he could tell me what had happened.

I though longingly of Erwin and the luxury carabinero stables with all their veterinary facilities. Pioneers cannot afford sentiment. In the wilds the knife or the bullet are the only practical medicines for very sick animals. It was only a horse, after all, they said, only a horse.

More days passed and even the kind-hearted Naomi began asking why I did not just leave Hornero and get another horse. Their owner, she pointed out, must have realized there was a risk of losing either one or both horses on a journey such a mine.

I decided to move my camp to the shore. Paddling might soothe the foot. The townsfolk said this was madness, and that the beach at night abounded in vagabonds, vagrants and thieves. I was more worried about the wind. I lashed the tent firmly between some bent trees near the beach and the partly overgrown hull of a derelict fishing boat. There was a great hole in the port side, large enough, I thought, to lead Hornero and Jolgorio through. I set to work cleaning the

133

inside of the old hull, removing loose bits of wood, knocking any sharp objects flat with my hammer and laying down a thick bed of clean silver sand. An hour later found the horses snug inside their new stable, happily munching a pile of freshly gathered bamboo leaves. I later moved the tent in as well, elated at this small triumph and listening smugly to the sound of the rain beating down outside. Noah, I thought, had certainly had the right idea!

By afternoon the weather had improved enough for me to take Hornero swimming. I felt new hope as he cantered in slow motion underwater, the poor hoof free of the burden of his weight, his tail chased by schools of tiny fishes. Dusk came and the sun appeared for the first time for a week, a solid orange ball that soon sank behind the horizon. I saddled Jolgorio and made one last expedition along the beach to gather driftwood. When I returned a campfire was already blazing in front of my hull. A group of very old men were sitting round it in tattered ponchos, stirring a saucepan.

'*Hola*,' I ventured nervously.

They looked up with bright eyes and thin faces and shuffled to make a place for me by the fire. One of them handed me a plate of what turned out to be fish and potato stew. I remembered the townspeople's warning. But fear is instinctive and I did not feel any towards these old men.

'We heard about you,' one of them explained, 'and have come to look after you – because you are a vagabond, a *pata de perra* like us.' He made it sound the finest thing in the world to be.

Inside the hull my sleeping-bag and all my clothes had been carefully hung up and Hornero supplied with a fresh pile of leaves to eat. They had also made a sort of mud poultice for his foot.

Over the next week these kindly old men, who all apparently lived in little huts along the shore, taught me how to dry fish and to cook seaweed. How to oil my clothes against the weather. How to build a good fire even while it was raining. They enthusiastically applauded my first clumsy efforts to do these things for myself, and night after night, sitting around the fire, eating our fish and sipping *mate* or rough red wine, they boasted of their protégée, their own very special gringa. Nobody could have had better friends or teachers. As they talked I began to learn a little more about them, and what extraordinary men they were.

There was José Miguel whose legs had been crushed by a falling tree while he had been cutting hardwood in the great forests further south. As soon as he had partially recovered he had rowed over two hundred kilometres north to Chaitén, looking for work. He now manoeuvred himself around in a little trolley designed by himself, and made a living carving animals out of driftwood for the tourists.

Ninety-year-old Emmanuel López told how a quarter of a century before he had escaped from a prison island in Magallanes, while serving a life sentence for a murder he had not committed. More recently he had escaped from the old people's home in Chaitén. 'I like to have the sky above me', he explained almost ruefully. 'Captivity is worse than any other hardship.'

Arturo was an old Cape Horner, his back twisted after falling from the mast on one of the last great trading sailing ships. He told me how he had once been flogged for starting a mutiny against a corrupt captain.

Another week passed and Hornero's foot was no better. The horse nurse had been adamant that there was no infection, yet in spite of all the care and paddling the hoof got hotter. 'Maybe you had better send for the nurse again,' one of the old men suggested.

The nurse arrived with three of his friends. They all examined Hornero. 'There is no doubt now that he has broken a bone,' the old man pronounced. Just then a vagabond I had not met before came staggering up. He was very drunk. He propped himself against Hornero's side for support, lifted the hoof gently and examined it.

'No, no, Señor,' he told the horse nurse. 'All that is wrong with this horse is that he has been pricked by a nail.'

'Stupid old man!' the nurse and his friends exclaimed, giving the drunk a shove. 'It's best to shoot your horse,' they said. 'We'll sell you another one.'

I looked at the nurse. Despite his bland face and sympathetic smile there was an expression in his eyes that was either guilt or fear.

The wind, the torrential rain, the electric storm were no more than red herrings. I recalled Hornero's dislike of the man. His nervousness while being shod. His restlessness afterwards. And the great haste with which the nurse had taken the shoes off again once Hornero had been discovered lame. I lifted the hoof and examined it for the hundredth time. As usual there was no sign of anything, no evidence. Taking a chance, knowing if I was wrong I would only be causing further damage, I got out my knife and pared away the edge of the hoof to the boundary line between sensitive and insensitive – and there it was, a small festering nailhole. No nail of course, just a quick prick done in seconds, the damage almost undiagnosable, but possibly deciding Hornero's whole future.

When I looked up again the horse nurse had gone. I realized he had known all along what was wrong with Hornero.

A week before, one of the tourists had been so touched by our plight that he had promised to send a parcel of disinflammatory injection serum and cream on his way back north to Santiago. It had arrived by plane carefully wrapped up in stout green paper, aptly addressed to 'La Loca Gringa, Chaitén'. If only the horse had been able to tell me what was the matter, my good Samaritan could have sent antibiotics and Hornero might have been cured by now. But the blame was all mine. I should have noticed how the horse nurse had sweated as he worked. That he was old and clumsy. That his tools were just a little bit rusty. That the card he had shown me to prove that he was a fine blacksmith and horse nurse was frayed and yellowing.

My meagre supply of penicillin would not go far. The hospital rather grudgingly sold me a little streptomycin designed for human use. But it needed ten of the tiny phials to make up one dose for Hornero. It was no use trying to ask General Mendoza for assistance. There were police here and they were quite friendly, but Chaitén was even more isolated than Chiloé and I was too deep in the thick fringes of the wilderness for a message to get through. Besides, Chaitén was ruled not by the police but by the military, who had been commissioned by President Pinochet to build the new road. There was no alternative but to try and get to the cavalry squadron in Santa Lucía, about sixty kilometres away. There would be sure to be a good vet there. But could Hornero make it?

It was worth one last effort, before the infection became even worse. I managed to shoe three of his feet. The sore one was a problem, for everybody warned me that the freshly blasted track to Santa Lucía was full of very sharp stones. Arturo the Cape Horner had an idea. That same evening he arrived back rolling an old tyre. 'We shall make your horse a moccasin,' he announced, and set to work with his knife.

By the end of the night they had made him a walking boot. The sides were made out of one of my cotton shirts with pouches for cottonwool which I could soak in the many rivers they said we would meet on our way, to keep the hoof cool. The sole was thick rubber to protect the hoof against the stones.

The next morning I said farewell to my friends and left Chaitén. As soon as we were outside the town we entered virgin forest. Even my anxiety about Hornero could not diminish my awe at the dramatic terrain. Great mountains rose up from foundations of impenetrable jungle just a few feet from the sides of the narrow track. The rocksides were so steep that sometimes the clinging trees stuck out almost at right angles.

This was the Austral track, the first land link between Chaitén and Santa Lucía. Despite costing between 80,000 and 160,000 dollars per kilometre to construct, it was still only a very rough stony track. The forests on its route had been so thick that breaches had been made with a combination of machetes, power saws and dynamite. Yet in spite of all the evidence of raw, freshly-blasted lumps of rock, the road did not seem real, not part of the wilderness around me, but merely an illusion pasted onto a landscape no human would ever really have the power to change.

Hornero hobbled along bravely and we made much better progress than I had expected, in spite of stopping to rest and paddle in nearly all the many streams and rivers along our way. My depression lifted now that we were on the move again. Somehow ''im up there' seemed to be back on our side. Even the rain stopped for a while. For the first time for many days I could see the tops of the mountains.

We passed the Yelcho Valley and Puerto Cardenas, arriving at Lago Yelcho just after dusk on the second day after leaving Chaitén. We crossed the lake at night on a raft. 'All you have to do is to keep going,' I kept telling Hornero. 'It is your only chance. Soon things will be better. I promise. I promise . . . '

Three days later we finally arrived at the tiny settlement of Villa Santa Lucía. Snowy glaciers rose above forest which had the wild, unkempt appearance of hair which has never been trimmed or looked after, wild and bushy, full of dead bits and broken ends. Almost as an afterthought amid all this wildness was a sprawl of little huts and houses. To one side, in front of the mountains, white sentry towers guarded the entrance of what looked like a Foreign Legion fort. This was our goal, the headquarters of the Villa Santa Lucía Cavalry Squadron.

I made my way rather nervously towards this impressive-looking establishment, clutching the horses' heads close to

138

me for moral support. Then I announced myself to the sentries and asked to see their commanding officer.

We were made very welcome. The horses were dealt with first, being ushered into a brand new stable and given hay and concentrated horse nuts and a bed of deep clean straw. Jolgorio quickly took command of the situation, bravely nipping the large cavalry horse in the next stall when he seemed too interested in their supply of food. 'Eating cures most problems' was his philosophy and he set to work putting it into practice.

'The grey horse has been pricked by a nail,' the squadron vet said as soon as he looked at Hornero's hoof. He told me that had I not struggled to Santa Lucía, and the required treatment of a heavy course of antibiotics further delayed, my horse would have lost all the horn of his hoof and have been useless for the next year and a half.

'Don't be upset,' he added when he saw my expression. 'We'll probably be able to put it right here.'

The acting commander of the barracks confirmed that the horses were most welcome to stay until Hornero was well again. 'There is only one problem, *uno problema*,' he added hesitantly, looking slightly embarrassed. 'This is strictly an all-male establishment, though you may come and see the horses as often as you like, of course.'

I told him that one of my most important rules was to try to live in my tent whenever possible and that I would be very comfortable. This was not quite true. My campsite by the banks of Río Frío was very beautiful and the weather suddenly was much warmer, but the next weeks were very difficult.

As usual it was completely my own fault. The problem was the soggy bundle of traveller's cheques which lay at the bottom of one of my green rucksacks. While in Puerto Montt and the world of banks, I had somehow not been able to contemplate such an emergency as Hornero's foot and simply had not cashed enough money. Life in Chaitén, trying out

139

useless remedies for my horse, had been expensive and I had spent much more time there than expected. Yet there, as here in Santa Lucía, one could more easily exchange a stone for money than one could a traveller's cheque from Barclay's Bank.

I could not bring myself to ask the soldiers for more help. Visions of little Jolgorio stuffing himself with horse nuts, of Hornero at last receiving the treatment he so desperately needed from a kindly and expert vet, comforted me each night as I curled up in my sleeping-bag. The squadron was doing quite enough. So instead I became absorbed in a series of interesting if foolhardy experiments.

I was not afraid of hunger. On my transatlantic crossing in *Fiesta Girl* the little boat had been too small to carry enough stores for the seventy days the voyage eventually had taken and I had completely run out of food almost a week before reaching New York. It hadn't done me any real harm. I decided to live off the land, roaming the river banks looking for things to eat. What would poison me and what would not? I wished I'd had a commando's training. I did not know how long I would be in Santa Lucía, but even after Hornero became better it would be at least two more weeks before I reached Coihaique and could cash a cheque. This journey might be tough and I felt it a good idea to get myself in training.

Words from some half-forgotten survival manual I had once read came back: 'Most seeds are edible if cooked. Most roots are edible if cooked. Most blue-coloured berries are edible. Beware of plants with milky sap. Beware of plants or mushrooms you cannot positively identify. Anything that swims, crawls, flies or walks has edible muscle portions.' 'Ugh!' I thought, for the time being confining myself to picking dandelion leaves which I knew people used for salads. I also tried to remember what the horses usually chose while grazing and to copy them.

I tried fishing, but most of the fish in Río Frío had been

140

frightened away by the recent blasting. I tried snaring, but all I caught was an old hen, which I shamefacedly returned to the poor settlers who owned it. My only real success was to discover a bush of ripe wild raspberries. It did not last long. In the end I spent my very last few pesos on a bag of flour from the rickety village store, put half aside for the long journey to Coihaique, and settled down to a diet consisting almost entirely of dandelion dumplings. I even felt quite well on it, or perhaps it was because my hopes were rising again: every day Hornero was getting better.

On 9 February I took Hornero for a ride up a mountain to test him. He seemed fit and well. But the journey between Santa Lucía and Coihaique would, I knew, be a very tough one. I looked at the horse and tried to work out how he felt. Would he want to carry on? Or should I send him back to the hacienda and go on with Jolgorio alone?

When we got back to the squadron stables, Jolgorio, for once ignoring his food, was plunging and neighing. He had been afraid that it was he that was being left behind. That made up my mind. 'We stick together!' I told them. But I decided that Hornero would carry only his saddle. I would walk. I would not chance the hoof going wrong again, by riding him too soon. In the health of that one hoof lay all my hopes and dreams, after all. In that hoof was the future.

At last, on 13 February, Don Luis, the cavalry vet, gave the all clear. Marcelo Hernández, the Squadron's acting commanding officer, and no less than a dozen young soldiers all helped load Jolgorio, adding stores of coffee, sugar, oil, dried meat and flour as gifts. This touched my heart and would make all the difference to the journey. Then we set off on the long, long road to Coihaique with me leading Jolgorio and Hornero walking jauntily behind.

Despite the fact that as soon as I sat down for lunch I was bitten by three mosquitoes and several forest leeches – which taught me never to sit down with bare legs again – I felt ecstatic. Hornero's hoof had stayed cool and well throughout the morning's march. The no man's land between success and failure seemed to be over at long last. The expedition had come alive again. 'We might,' I thought, 'make it to Cape Horn after all.'

Chapter Thirteen

All though our journey my tent had won me many friends. The rich people had thought it fun. The poor had felt at home in it because as a dwelling it was even more humble than the smallest shack they lived in. Children had enjoyed playing games in it. Hens, pigs, foxes, an owl with a broken wing, a little calf, as well as a multitude of cats and dogs, had all at different times arrived as uninvited guests. However, the grandest visitor I ever had appeared on our first night out from Villa Santa Lucía, 13 February.

All day long it had rained and rained as we marched along. Trying to escape the torrents I had used my machete to cut through the undergrowth and to fight our way deep into the relative shelter of the forest, pitching my tent at dusk in a part that was so dense I could no longer see the sky. Even so, our campsite was still very wet and uncomfortable and the horses, tied to branches nearby, looked nervous and miserable. I could see they were missing the luxury of the cavalry stables. Despite this, I soon fell asleep. Somehow if the hardness of the day matches the hardness of the night, sleep is never a problem, no matter how bad the discomfort.

In the middle of the night a slight noise inside my tent woke me. I turned to find myself looking into a pair of large orange eyes. My own eyes, when they became accustomed to the dark, made out the shape of what seemed to be a very large cat. It was about four feet long – the size, I suddenly realized, of a puma.

A puma! My head spun with excitement, more excitement really than apprehension, and I clutched the edge of my sleeping-bag, trying to stay completely still. All I had ever heard about pumas went rushing through my mind. Short of mythology and legend, there seemed to be more stories about the puma than about any other South America animal. The Mapuche Indians admired the *pangui*, as they called him, for his intelligence and strength. The Argentinian gauchos had recognized the puma's courage in taking on and often killing the far larger jaguar. Yet there were many stories of pumas shedding real tears when cornered by human hunters, refusing to defend themselves. It was said they never attacked a human, even a child. Mike Andrews, I remembered, had written a very good 'defence' of the puma in his book *The Flight of the Condor*, including a tale of a young woman who in the sixteenth century had been condemned for treachery and left to die tied to a tree. Her captors had returned the following day expecting to find her bones picked clean. But to their amazement she had been without even a scratch. She explained that pumas had come to her aid and defended her against other wild beasts – whereupon, the story went, she'd been instantly released.

More than one naturalist had verified this extraordinary affinity the puma has with man. He is totally without the treacherous nature of other large wild cats. However, all the puma's virtues could not disguise his appetite, it was said, for sheep, young cattle and even for young horses. Farmers hated him and the latest handbook I had read on wildlife in Chile stated: 'You will be very lucky to see him. Being ruthlessly hunted has made the puma very wary and scarce . . . ' So I sat there utterly still, feeling numb, damp and extremely privileged.

Tawny-coloured and huge, my visitor appeared to be quite relaxed, licking his paws, unaware of my presence. I longed to be able to switch on my torch to see him better. Instead I crouched rigid. My muscles cramped with the effort of trying

144

to stay still. Maybe I should have chased him away and gone out to check the horses, but some instinct told me that he had not harmed them. More than anything else I wanted him to stay till morning so that I might see him better. But eventually a spasm of cramp forced me to move and my visitor sprang into the air with such violence that he nearly took the whole tent with him, and dashed out into the night.

The horses had gone too. They had actually broken the stout branches they had been tied to. I put on more clothes, got out my flashlight and went in search of them. They had not got far, and were completely unharmed, but were all caught up in undergrowth. Jolgorio had recovered his equanimity enough to be busy eating the leaves off the broken branch he had been trailing from the end of his headcollar.

Having soothed the horses and remoored them, I retired once more to my damp sleeping-bag and tried to go to sleep. Every time I dozed off, my dreams were filled with large animals with golden eyes and tawny fur, licking their paws. Sometimes these would turn into mere marmalade cats. Then as I reached out to stroke them, they would become huge again. I would raise my machete and they'd look at me pleadingly, golden tears filling golden eyes.

First daylight showed my tent flap to be torn and one of the aluminium tent poles to be badly bent. My sugar supply had been opened and some of my coffee scattered. The bag of dried *charqui* meat which the soldiers had given me for the journey, had vanished. It was a small price to pay for an extraordinary experience.

Maybe it was because my little green home was really more like a naturalist's 'hide' than a tent, that creatures felt so at home in it. But not all were as welcome as the puma. I had woken up with a feeling of numbness in my feet and a terrible ache in my legs, attributing this at first to sleeping in such damp surroundings. 'That's it! I thought. 'My grandmother's arthritis coming on already. Well if anyone really deserves to get it, it's me for sleeping wet through . . . '

But arthritis was not the problem. As I prised my legs out of the sleeping-bag, I discovered them be covered with what looked like fat black grapes, a whole vineyard of them. But these 'grapes' had suckers. Bloated and horrific-looking, it was only by the twin hooks near their heads that I recognized them to be the same breed as the slim, lively, slug-textured leeches I had pulled off my legs during our lunchtime picnic in the forest the day before.

My first reaction was one of repulsion. I wanted to brush them off, pull them out. Somehow, just to be rid of them quickly. No good. Yesterday's bites had not been many, but they were already turning septic, and I realized that by pulling them off I had left some of the leeches' hooks behind in my skin.

I had read somewhere that the way to get rid of leeches is to burn them off with a cigarette. What cigarette? What about matches instead? I tried it and immediately yelled in pain. The leech just clung on, looking fatter than ever, as though the heat of the flame had merely made him much thirstier and he'd had to take another gulp of my blood. I had another try. Again no success.

Eventually a gleam of inspiration sent me rummaging into the depths of one of the green rucksacks looking for Dai Bowen's bottle of local anaesthetic serum. It did the trick. With my skin slightly numb I managed to hold the match near the head of each leech long enough to make it drop off. No doubt the survival manuals would advise that leeches are edible wild food and that I should have boiled them for lunch. I have to admit that I simply buried the little monsters.

Getting rid of the night's haul of leeches was to become part of my regular morning routine while in the rain forest, as was painting my and the horses' legs with some strong and hopefully nasty-tasting disinfectant before retiring. This worked very well indeed for the horses. But the little beasts seemed to consider me a delicacy worth any amount of trouble. How they managed to get into my sleeping-bag night after night I'll never know. In the end, the best remedy seemed to be the right mental attitude. The bites were not serious, after all. Soon they ceased to bother me, and I became quite pleased, even blasé, about my lack of queasiness.

Having got rid of that first crop of leeches after the eventful night of 13 February, I sat in my tent for a while, waiting for the weather to clear. Rain like that should have been temporary. Instead it went on and on. I realized that if I just waited for it to stop, I might wait forever. I usually put the tent away first, so that I could move freely in order to pack away all the possessions which had been underneath. But now everything had somehow to be packed while I was still inside the tent, with the igloo being taken down last thing of all. The spilt sugar had converted itself into syrup. All my other belongings were a damp, soggy mess. I tried not to look too closely as I packed, simply designating one rucksack as the 'wet' rucksack into which I crammed everything already wet beyond redemption. The other one I lined with yet more plastic bags and into this I packed all equipment which might optimisically be labelled 'dry'. In Chaitén and Santa Lucía I had become quite used to living in my tent in the rain with a fair degree of comfort. It was making the transition from campsite to four-footed mobile home which was so difficult. Worst of all was trying to fold six soaking blankets on Jolgorio's soaking back. The slippery packsaddle. The slippery straps and girth. The general confusion was accentuated by the noise of the rain as it crashed down in torrents through the branches.

It was a great relief to get back on the Austral track and be on the move again. As we made our way south towards the ferry point on Río Palena, on either side of us rose high rocky cliffs muffled by ancient trees resembling oaks. Some of the trees were bright with 'Quintral', the pretty species of

147

parasitic mistletoe after which René Varas', famous horse had been named. I began to feel more cheerful with every step I took, especially because there was no sign of Hornero's lameness returning. The ache in my feet was less than the ache in my conscience would have been had I ridden him. My reward was that free of any load, he actually seemed happy, walking jauntily behind, both he and Jolgorio chomping at the bamboo undergrowth as we passed.

The force of the rain did not alter, but my feelings about it certainly did. It really was wonderful how feelings could change, get better by themselves, without one having to do anything about them, or alter any circumstances. Most of all there was something wonderful about walking on my own two feet. They were covered in blisters, but I felt good, confident. I was walking in wet socks. My trousers too felt wet. But my sombrero kept the rain from actually dripping into my eyes and the rain ran off my poncho, not letting much through. The walking kept me warm. I felt fit, happy and stronger than I had been since breaking my ribs. Really I was walking for my own sake as well as Hornero's. With every step I was building up a little more stamina, a little more insurance against the moment when I got to a region still further south where there were no roads and I would have to walk. And as Bruce Chatwin had written in *In Patagonia*, 'If you walk furiously enough, you don't need any other religion.'

At midday the rain actually stopped for a while and the sun came out. Maybe it was because it was so rare, or maybe it was just the wonderful intoxicating smell of the sun's gentle warmth on the wet forest, but somehow the sunshine seemed of a different quality to that found elsewhere in the world.

I stopped for a break near a river crashing down from the snowy glacier far above us in a series of spectacular waterfalls, providing icy water with which to bathe the horses' feet. The invalid Hornero I actually tethered in the middle of the stream, hoping that the clear, cold water might soothe his

148

bad foot. When I got out the remains of my bread, a flock of brilliant green-and-scarlet parrots arrived, sharing my picnic with the enthusiasm of an English sparrow. Along the river bank were thick clumps of purple flowers, a variety I had not seen before. They looked so beautiful and delicate that I was certain they had opened only minutes before when the sun came out. Among the flowers flitted dozens of tiny little hummingbirds with bright green backs.

Like all visits to paradise, it was short. Soon it began to rain again, as solidly and furiously as ever. But the rain no longer upset me. It was not an enemy. It was as much a part of the forest as the flowers and the birds.

> 'The woods are lovely dark and deep,
> But I have promises to keep,
> And miles to go before I sleep . . . '

The horses bent their ears back as I strode along reciting poetry to them. There were no huts or settlements along the track, just an endless line of dark green trees on either side. All day my only contacts with humanity were occasional jeeps carrying the new breed of Chilean visitor to the south. One of these slowed down and a lady passed me a newly-baked chocolate cake out of the car window. She and her family obviously thought me completely mad, walking on and on in front of two horses in the pouring rain.

I was travelling the same road as these friendly people, but living in a different world. As in the desert, travelling very slowly with two horses polarized life into extremely bad and extremely good experiences. No moment of the entire seven months that my expedition had taken so far had been bland, now even less so.

Probably the lady in the jeep had never had to cope with leeches, or with sleeping alone in the forest wet through. Probably she had not had to put on wet socks that morning. But had she seen a puma? Had she had wild parrots share her lunch? The jeep might offer protection. But could it offer the rich smells and scents of the forest as it hurtled along? Or that special sort of silence through which, if one listened very carefully, it was possible to hear the creatures of the forest canopy going about their daily life?

In the very inconvenience of my way of travelling, in the fact that I rarely travelled from the sanctuary of one settlement to another, but had to stop wherever I happened to be when darkness fell, lay the heart of the whole expedition. I could never tell what might happen in this strange brantub dip of fate.

In spite of walking as briskly as possible for the rest of that day, I did not manage to get to the Palena ferry, or to the little settlement of La Junta just beyond, before nightfall.

It is always a mistake to keep on travelling after dark – not because it is impossible to travel at night, but because if you get tired and want to stop it is very difficult to find a suitable campsite when you cannot see where you are. That night it was pitch black by the time I decided to take the horses off the track and make camp.

I tried to lead them forward. Jolgorio dug his toes in and wouldn't budge. Hornero wouldn't move more than a few feet away from the track. 'You pigs,' I told them, regretting I could not lead them and whack them from behind at the same time. 'Why are you doing this? You have never done this before. Was it all the poetry?'

Utterly exhausted after the long day I managed to drag them a little way into the forest and tied them up. I put up the tent and collapsed into my sleeping-bag. All night long the tent writhed and shook under the force of the wind and the rain.

When dawn came I found I had been camped just two feet away from a precipice with a fifty-foot drop to the swamp below.

Chapter Fourteen

My forward tentpegs were clawing away at the crumbling edges of a thin shelf of rocky earth overhanging the cliff itself. The ground under my tent, it was clear, could collapse at any moment. To move at all might bring disaster. Yet somehow I had to reach the rucksacks and saddles which I had stowed as usual under a tarpaulin in front of the tent – just out of reach.

The very thumping of my heart seemed enough to bring about catastrophe. I looked longingly back to where I had tied the horses when they had refused to come any further. 'I've spent so much time teaching them to trust me,' I thought despairingly. 'Whenever will I learn to trust them?'

For many minutes I sat as still as possible, just trying to think what to do. I was sure that if I once left the tent and went to try to tie a safety line between the trees and myself, that I would lose the tent and all my equipment. I would never be able to get back onto the ledge again without it collapsing. So instead I finally attached myself to a rather insecure-looking thorn bush nearby and inched myself forward. An inferno of thorns and swamp far below spun before me as I gazed dizzily down. The stone of the cliff itself was a dark grey colour which made the patches of scarlet moss growing in its cracks seem even more dramatic, and for a moment it was not moss at all, but the blood of former victims of the cliff which had been spilt there. 'If I fall,' I thought, 'nobody will ever rescue me. No one will even discover where my bones are.'

Perhaps this made me extra careful, because eventually, with the exception of one tent peg which I just had to cut free, I managed to retrieve everything, more or less intact, except for my torn nerves. Shakily I packed up Jolgorio. Then the horses and I made our way across the Palena and Rosselot rivers on the road contractors' rickety ferries, and by evening had arrived at the tiny settlement of La Junta.

La Junta was like an island in the green rain forest, far inland of the actual sea. Until very recently it had been almost impossible to get to. Its only link with the rest of the world had been via the turbulent Río Palena itself, which like most southern Chilean rivers is very difficult and dangerous to navigate.

The little brown wooden houses, some built out of plain pine, some out of Alerce shingles, a wood much valued because it is water repellent, gave the impression of a jumbled mixture of cultures. So did the inhabitants. They explained that some of the families were descended from Argentinians, who had floated downstream on the Río Palena which had its source in their country. They had never got round to struggling back upstream again and so had settled here. Others were descended from Chilote Indians, who, having somehow managed to make the voyage from Chiloé to the mainland in their little open boats, had refused to be daunted by the furious river, and had inched their way up to this point. There were also some descendants of fierce Araucanians who had come south to escape persecution by the Spanish.

One of these was Don Jorge who ushered my horses into a small paddock with lots of tall grass. That it had begun raining again did not seem to matter so much for their coats had been growing rapidly and now they did not seem to mind the weather. When they had been settled, he took me off to meet his family. 'We have a restaurant now for the new visitors, but the kitchen is for friends,' his wife said with a smile. One of her many daughters produced a sort of wrap

152

and made it clear I should take off my soaking clothes, which were immediately washed and hung up among the joints of smoky *charqui* meat on the ceiling to dry, while they served me delicious casserole and red wine.

Don Jorge's black eyes gleamed above his high cheekbones as he told me how his great grandfather had escaped from the Spaniards by rowing hundreds of miles south in a tiny boat with his wife and five small children. The Spaniards had been especially eager to kill them, having discovered that the family was related to the great Araucanian warrior Galvarino, who had engaged in endless battles against the conquistadors. When they eventually captured Galvarino the Spanish severed his right forearm. But in spite of this terrible handicap he had managed to escape and had gone on fighting against the invaders by means of a pointed lance attached to his elbow.

Recently the population of La Junta had expanded dramatically as road contractors with giant yellow machines and matching yellow oilskins had arrived from the north, followed by the first officials, policemen and tourists. While the original pioneering inhabitants absorbed changes with an easy adaptability taught by a hundred years of hardship, they had not yet become used to the fact that it was now possible to get to their little settlement much more easily than before. Every traveller was still fêted as though he had spent weeks dragging a boat upriver to get there.

Next day I sadly said goodbye to La Junta. Don Jorge, who had been horrified at my story about camping on the edge of a precipice, warned me not to leave the track again. The reason that for centuries the only access to La Junta had been by river was because even the Indians considered the jungle in this region particularly treacherous, and did not try to get through with horses. 'You're lucky to be alive,' he said. 'Stay on the road.'

LOG: *16 February 1985; south of La Junta, camped beside Lago Risopatrón, a little way off the track*
The horses and I have spent a most peaceful night here. Now I'm enjoying breakfast of bread and coffee watching rare early-morning sunlight creep across the water and the trees, a kaleidoscope of colours approaching, one foot, two foot, nearer and nearer. The sun is sparkling in the dew hung on enormous cobwebs laced among the bushes. Looking at the forest spiders' patient and perfect work, I feel they could teach me a lot about pitching my tent securely. From time to time I have to move my position, circling round my fire to avoid the smoke in the light variable wind. I'm lucky with the fire this morning. Since my introduction to archipelago-type weather in Chaitén, I have got into the habit of taking small twigs and bits of wood to bed with me, or at least into the tent, in an attempt to dry them – so that I may persuade a reluctant campfire to light in the mornings. This however does not always work. Campfires, like banks, rarely do what you want when you most need them to . . .

The following day found us approaching the picturesque tiny settlement of Puerto Puyuguapi, known for its German-style architecture, its thermal baths, and for having at least 3810 millimetres of rainfall a year.

LOG: *17 February 1985*
My first sight of the sea since Chaitén, but I hardly appreciated it because my feet were hurting so much, my shoes having given me a great deal of trouble on these last few kilometres to Puyuguapi. I truly understand now why even the horses' iron shoes have needed changing so often and how hard the journey really has been on them. Since Santa Lucía my shoes have developed holes in their toes, and have broken down on both sides thanks to all the walking I am now doing. My main

problem is not that water squelches ceaselessly in one end and out the other, but that mud and small stones also find their way in and encrust themselves painfully upon my socks.

Often I have thought, 'I might get into the *Guinness Book of Records* when it comes to making mistakes.' One of the greatest of these had been early in my journey when I had been riding most of the time and it had been too hot to wear my original magnificent walking boots: I had sent them ahead of me to Puerto Montt for use in the south. They had never arrived. Later it transpired that they too had spent most of my journey on the move, being sent backwards and forwards on buses, but never arriving where I was. Lucky Leslie's Patagonian walking boots had had to be sent back, in spite of their sentimental value and their Patagonian spirit; they really had been too big for me. So when I arrived in Puyuguapi, my own footwear – as opposed to the horses' – was now my major worry. It did not last long. The kindly people I met there bestowed upon me a large pair of white tennis shoes, not new but sound. So I said goodbye to my faithful old shoes, which had been worn out by all the walking on rough terrain. I took a sentimental photo of them before I threw them away.

The friendly welcome I received in these little settlements accentuated my isolation and solitude on the journey between them. There were times when the road seemed very long and I felt very alone indeed.

Perhaps the worst of such moments occurred on 20 February. We had left Puyuguapi and were ambling peacefully between the usual deep green trees, their trunks couched with thick bamboo undergrowth. I was feeling happy because Hornero was showing no sign of lameness, and we seemed to be coping with everything better than before.

Suddenly, from out of the undergrowth leapt a man. Gibbering in a high piping voice, his head held at a strange

155

angle, he snatched Jolgorio's headcollar and plunged back into the undergrowth dragging my poor horse with him! I was so surprised I simply stood transfixed.

Luckily Hornero, who had been following along nonchalantly, still enjoying his holiday, had been forgotten in the flurry. Now he was standing looking puzzled as if he did not know whether he was meant to follow Jolgorio or not. As I jumped onto his back and urged him into the jungle, I realized that the horses' green drinking bowl had been tied to the man's own saddle as though it were some trophy. I had been unable to find it when breaking camp that morning. He must have been following us all that time.

Hornero and I struggled through the thick undergrowth for nearly an hour. I was crying with anxiety and anger when Hornero suddenly stopped, pricked his ears and gave a loud whinny. Then I heard it too. Somewhere, quite a long way off, Jolgorio was neighing piteously. It sounded like a scream and my insides clenched with dread – Hornero's too apparently, for off he set. There was no possibility of riding now for the undergrowth was too thick, so I just clung on to the reins and to the lower part of his mane, and was more or less dragged along.

Suddenly we saw him. He had fallen into a deep ditch. One of his hind legs was twisted up behind him. His head was wedged at an unnatural angle against the roots of a tree. The man who had stolen him was screaming and beating him mercilessly, trying to make him get out. I had never seen such a look in Jolgorio's eyes before. Indeed, I had never seen such a look of misery and pain in any animal's eyes. I rushed forward, out of my mind with fury, and set about the man. He paid no attention and went on screaming at Jolgorio. At that moment it occurred to me that he wasn't simply a horse-thief. He was quite obviously deranged.

I looked around for another weapon, wishing that my machete wasn't in Jolgorio's pack. Then I remembered the purple veterinary spray I always carried on me as first aid against minor cuts and scratches. I pointed it straight at the madman's eyes and pressed the button. For a moment I thought he was going to explode. His face went bright red before the spray turned it purple. He gave a loud scream, clutched at his eyes, and dropped his stick. I continued my attack, emptying the whole canister over him. He gave a sort of howl like a wolf, and fled into the trees.

Silence fell over the forest. The frogs, whose croaks normally provided a constant background hum, had gone quiet. Even the birds had stopped singing. I felt terribly alone and utterly helpless. I suddenly realized how far we were from the track. I could shout and shout and no one would hear me. I strained my ears for a noise that would tell me that the madman was lurking nearby. But all I could hear was the beating of my heart. For a moment I even wondered if I'd imagined him. Then Jolgorio gave a little groan and I knew that he had been very real indeed and that my problems had only just begun.

He was stuck firmly in the ditch. I stroked his head, murmuring 'Jolgorio, Jolgorito,' in as soothing a tone as I could muster. Then I took all the equipment off his back and filled the ditch with leaves and twigs to give him some foothold. It didn't work. The packs I had retrieved contained my spare ropes. With great difficulty I got one rope under his belly and one under his hind quarters. Then I put several of the saddle-blankets under the whole of the underneath of his belly so that the ropes would not cut him too much. At the end of my transatlantic voyage, when I was weak with hunger, I had at last discovered the great value of makeshift blocks and tackles, which had meant I could pull a sail in with minimum effort. Now I desperately tried to work out how I could make the same technique help Jolgorio. In the end I ran a rope from Jolgorio round a tree then back to a loop half-way along its length, hoping I had thereby created some sort of makeshift block and tackle to give extra purchase or pulling power. Then I tied the end onto Hornero's girth.

157

'Pull!' I begged him. He plunged and struggled gamely, but to little avail. Jolgorio still seemed completely stricken.

I felt close to tears. Hornero and Jolgorio weren't just horses, they were my partners. If anything my desperation to save Jolgorio was even greater than had he been a human partner.

'*Adelante*, Jolgorio, *adelante*!' I kept urging him.

I had almost given up when, with a great squelch, he staggered out and stood forlornly, steaming and quivering. He was covered in mud, as by now were Hornero and I, but otherwise seemed miraculously unscathed. I put my arms around his neck and hugged him.

I did not really dare to look at my packs and my equipment. My camera and the tape-recorder were coated with mud, but most of my possessions were intact. The only thing I could not find was the small bag containing my bread and other food supplies. I had no other food and no money to buy some at the next settlement, for the stores had been meant to last me the two hundred kilometres to Coihaique.

Still, I knew I could go many days without food if necessary. The immediate problem was that I was completely lost. Jolgorio, thank God, had not been injured, so I loaded the horses and we made our way through the forest till we arrived at a small stream where, after perfunctory attempts to wash off some of the mud, I put up the tent and went to sleep. There seemed no point worrying about the madman returning. There was not much I could do about it if he did. Remembering his face as he fled comforted me as I fell asleep.

I woke in the morning dizzy with hunger. The horses were lucky. There were plenty of bamboo shoots for them to eat. I watched them enviously, then we set off into the forest. I had lost my little compass earlier in the journey, and here in the forest it was quite impossible to see the direction of the sun on the rare occasions when it stopped raining. After several hours wandering blindly through the trees I came upon a small wooden hut.

As I knocked on the rickety door I couldn't get Walter de la Mare's poem out of my mind:

'Is there anybody there?' said the Traveller . . .

A dog with all its ribs showing rushed out and barked at us, but the family who emerged after it seemed friendly and pleased to see me. They were especially delighted by the horses. I tied up Hornero and Jolgorio outside and gave them some more bamboo leaves, then entered the hut. The Mamma, who had a squint which allowed her to look at both sides of the small cabin at once, seemed very cheerful and patted my head. Then she filled a very large pot with water and put it on the fire. The family were dressed in much the same clothes as the other country people I had met, and the little house could have been any of a hundred I had been in. But there was something peculiar here. My rumbling stomach told me what it was. There was no smell of cooking. Usually, in even the humblest homes in southern Chile, there was the ever-present aroma of a casserole simmering on the stove. Not here. A little girl, clutching the hem of her dress, was crying piteously in the corner. The men sat sullenly chewing empty pipes. Suddenly I realized that this family was suffering from acute hunger. 'If only I hadn't lost my stores,' I thought.

After we had sat for a while making half-understood small talk, one of the sons who had been shifting around rather impatiently got up and offered to go out and check the horses for me. I don't know what instinct made me follow him outside. I came upon him standing beside Jolgorio, holding his knife. He was busy paring away the longish hair near the horse's jugular vein.

I snatched the knife from his hands and stood there beside Jolgorio, trembling with fury. The young man shrank back against the walls of the shack.

Little Jolgorio seemed to be wondering what the matter was. He bent round, calmly nuzzling my shoulder and rubbing his nose on the rough wool of my poncho. I stroked

159

him, more to calm myself than anything else. Hornero stood a little way off, pulling his rope taut, ears laid back flat. The young man would certainly not still be standing upright, I thought, had he tried to touch *him*. Even in the drama of the situation, I was able to wonder at the difference in the horses. In spite of having been brought up together, one had been endowed with permanent mistrust of humans in his soul, the other permanent trust. In its own way, each was a threat to them.

By now the whole family had rushed out of the hut. They seemed as surprised as Jolgorio had been at how upset I was. They all started talking at once. They were very hungry, they explained. Even their children had no food. And I was hungry, too, wasn't I? What was wrong with eating one of the horses? I had another one. Yes, the brown horse had been destined for the pot, but the Señora insisted that they would have invited me to the supper and have made *charqui* out of whatever was left to keep me going on my journey. I flinched as she came up to me and began trying to stroke my hand, apparently to soothe me.

They really were very thin, with their bones visible under their clothes and huge brown eyes staring out of their thin faces. All at once my anger left me and was replaced by pity. What were the ethics of such a situation? Nobody who has not been truly hungry can ever really say what they would do, or what they would steal, if driven by desperation. If only I had some food to give them, I thought again. But I knew I hadn't and that the horses and I must leave at once. So I picked up the lead reins and made off back into the undergrowth. The family were still apparently too bewildered by my reaction to try to stop me leaving. They would never understand, and I could never explain, how the life of a horse could ever be worth more than the life of a hungry child.

160

Chapter Fifteen

After leaving the hut in the midst of the forest, I struggled on for several hours, then stopped beside a small stream, feeling sick and weak. Why had I not at least asked the destitute family for directions back to the Carretera Austral? I had completely lost my sense of direction. I was enclosed in a soft green womb from which there seemed no possibility of I or the horses ever escaping.

Then all at once I noticed that the large tree trunk fallen across the stream close to where I sat had little steps in it, leading across. These had obviously been etched deliberately with a sharp axe. On the other side the undergrowth hung like a solid wall. But at the bottom where the trunk ended was a tiny opening. I left the horses eating, and went to investigate.

After crawling a little way along this bamboo tunnel on my hands and knees I thought, 'I must have imagined the steps. I must really be going mad!' All that was happening as a result of my exploration was that I was becoming even muddier than before and badly scratched by the sharp bamboo stalks.

Gradually, however, the tunnel became wider, then opened up into a path. Then all at once a blinding light dazzled me through the trees ahead. It took some time for it to sink in that this was really only ordinary daylight amplified by my unaccustomed eyes. A few moments later I was leaning on a carefully-built wooden fence. It was no ordinary fence. It seemed specially built and braced to keep the entire

161

rain forest at bay. On one side the wilderness reigned; on the other, in a small clearing, stood a pretty little farm and homestead. Flowers which looked like pink roses climbed up the walls of the house and all around it grew a luxuriant profusion of beans, cabbages, maize and potatoes. A little further off was a large barn, and near this stood two sleek oxen tethered to each other with a wooden yoke. Several cows and calves were cropping the grass, and hens were pecking at the ground. On either side of the homestead were two smooth, almost miraculously green paddocks. I could see the scars where tree roots had been pulled out and their craters painstakingly filled in.

I gazed unbelieving at this extraordinary sight. My legs felt very weak. I was half determined to flee back into the forest again, grab my horses and get away. 'Don't be stupid. Don't be so stupid,' I told myself, holding onto the fence as though for moral support. 'You've met with nothing but kindness in Chile,' I reminded myself firmly. 'The last twenty-four hours were no more than an accident, a bad dream . . . '

It was too late to leave anyway. '*Hola . . . hola*!' a voice was calling. A tall man in a flowing black poncho and with a feather in his sombrero came striding across the fields towards me.

I stood rooted to the spot.

'*Soy Miguel*,' he said. He stretched out his hand and I knew he was a friend.

I must have looked a dreadful sight, muddy and bleeding from my scratches, with bits of moss and leaves in my hair and poncho. The tennis shoes I had been given in Puyuguapi were black with grime. But he smiled in a kindly way and seemed quite amused at my surprise at finding his farm. 'There are some of us in this forest whom nobody will ever see as they travel the new road,' he said. 'Yet really we are not so far away from it.'

He showed me how to bring my horses over to his farm by a slightly easier route than the one I had taken. Then he won my heart forever by letting the horses into one of his beautiful green paddocks to graze.

The kitchen bustled with activity. One of Miguel's daughters was making bread. Another was chopping cabbage. A third was strumming a guitar. A boy sat quietly carving a saddle out of a piece of raw wood. The lady of the house was slicing meat. When she saw me she dropped her knife and rushed over to embrace me. I felt like bursting into tears. An hour later I was sitting sleepy and content beside the fire, full of hot stew, wearing yet another borrowed shawl as all my wet things dried. I was back in paradise.

Miguel shook his head when he heard about my recent adventures. He explained that the government was trying to colonize the region by offering all sorts of inducements to would-be settlers. A man had only to arrive, put a fence around any unfenced land he chose, clear it of trees and undergrowth, and it became his property. He could get the deeds simply by sending a plan of what he had enclosed to the nearest town, in this case Coihaique. But the price in terms of hardship was very high.

'The rain forest is not a kind place,' he added. 'For those who do not succeed starvation or madness may never be far away. But,' and his eyes lit up, 'if you love freedom enough, everything is possible here. In the north I was a poor man. Now I have endless good water, endless firewood, a fine house which I built myself. Beautiful rich soil which has never grown crops before. I arrived here four years ago with my wife and three children, two cows and two skinny horses and some hens. Now I have five children, eight cows, two oxen which I have bred and trained myself and horses which are no longer skinny.'

Next morning the family insisted on loading me up with bread, sugar, cheese, dried meat and herbal *mate*. I felt overwhelmed. To say thank you was not enough – enough for them perhaps, but not for me. I had no money and they probably would not have accepted it anyway. What could I do? I muttered something about how I wished I could show my gratitude, but they hushed me. What would mean most to them, they said, would be a picture postcard from England, to be sent to their post box in Coihaique. They all wrote their names in my log book and I made them a promise that I would do this. But it might be months before I got back home. Something had to be done now.

I rummaged in one of the rucksacks, pulling out all my freshly packed possessions. Right at the bottom I found two pairs of bright red climbing socks which I had bought from Blacks of Greenock the previous June and had been saving for some emergency. The Señora's face softened with pleasure as she touched them. 'They're from so very far away,' she whispered.

LOG: *20 February 1985*
It's good to be 'unlost' and on our way due south again. We've just travelled along one of the most spectacular stretches of the whole journey so far. The road is etched insecurely into the side of the cliff itself. Water crashes from the cliff top to a foaming river far below, just missing the track itself. It's like being inside a waterfall. The mountains around us now are full of waterfalls – so many that it is as though the mountains themselves were actually filled with water and have merely been punctured in a hundred places. There have been dramatic changes in the terrain today, our path becoming much steeper, and the deep ocean of the rain forest shallower. More small settlements are becoming visible, also more jeeps on the road – altogether fewer leeches and trees, and more people.

One of the reasons for there being more settlers there was that we were nearing Puerto Aysén, which has easy access from the sea. The effects of this increased accessibility were not all good ones. The road now passed through areas of forest which had been utterly destroyed. It is so easy to burn

164

trees; so difficult to chop them down, especially without powered tools; thus hundreds of acres had been devastated by great forest fires, started deliberately by settlers before the turn of the century. They stood there still, a graveyard of burnt dead stumps.

The early settlers had been ruthless. Trees were the enemy and had to be destroyed. They had not even left a few standing to shelter their houses. More important, they had not thought about the long-term effects on the soil. The present-day colonists were not merely remorseful and guilty about the actions of their forebears, they were also very alarmed at the disastrous amount of soil erosion which had taken place. CONAF, Chile's national forestry commission, had made tremendous attempts to reforest some areas with carefully-guarded quick-growing pines. They had erected large signs along the Carretera Austral saying, 'Beware of Forest Fire', and little cartoons of squirrels saying, 'This is our home and your heritage, please look after it'. But it was a difficult task. Trees which were thousands of years old had been burned in hours, and could never be replaced. Worse than that, the wildlife – insects, birds, seedlings, worms – had also been destroyed, and with them the heart of the rich soil.

The tourists from Santiago were particularly scathing about the destruction caused by early settlers. 'What a mess they have left behind,' remarked the driver of a white van who had stopped on the track to chat to me. He looked rather doubtfully at my muddy camera and said he could let me have photos of the burnt forests if I needed them. 'What about the pollution in Santiago?' one of his companions rejoined. 'Without the excuse of hardship or ignorance, modern man destroys nature just as thoroughly by polluting the atmosphere.'

They dried my damp poncho and horse blankets on the bonnet of their van, and gave me whisky in a plastic cup to warm me up. A little while later I said goodbye to them and strode off, swaying slightly, with Hornero and Jolgorio following patiently behind.

As I got closer to Coihaique the land became better again, with bigger and more prosperous-looking farms along the way. One of the finest of these was Campo Grande, where we were welcomed warmly. Señor Juan Andrade ran his hands lovingly over Hornero's and Jolgorio's pedigree brandmarks. He too bred thoroughbred horses. Carefully watched by the fat white goat which was the family's mascot, he gave my horses a badly needed haircut, in order, as he put it, that we might arrive in town in style. He also presented me with some sheepskin chaps, which later were to save my life. Don Juan was not encouraging about the next stage of my journey. 'Don't go any further by land,' he advised. 'Up to now it has been fairly easy . . . '

On 27 February I arrived at long last at Coihaique, in the middle of the archipelago. Leaving the horses to nibble the grass in the main plaza, I rushed to the bank. Yes, there were some letters for me, and a little money. But I had arrived only just in time. One day more and they would have sent them all back to England. I tore open the letters from home, then burst into tears. Everyone I had left still loved me, but they wanted to know when I would be coming home. My bank was concerned about my overdraft. They all wanted me back. Yet they all depended on me finishing my job here successfully. The expedition had been meant to be completed by November 1984. It was now nearly March 1985, and I still had such a long way to go. It was no use worrying, I told myself firmly. Whatever was happening back home, there was nothing I could do about it. I must learn to worry only about the things I could do something about, such as getting ready in the most efficient way possible for the next stage of the expedition.

Coihaique was a beautiful place. It looked like the average Chilean town, with the same plazas, banks, shops, hair salons, the same local radio station. But what made it special were the snowcapped mountains all around and the crisp clean air. The weather here was much sharper and colder than I had become used to, with much less rain. Suddenly I was glad to be out of the rain forest.

And in a country where I had been shown unlimited kindness, Coihaique was also special for its people. The mayor welcomed me warmly. So did the local chief of police. The town's chief pharmacist offered me a campsite in his garden, while the head of the local agricultural college gave hospitality to my horses, and arranged for the best black-smith he knew of to come and reshoe them with specially-made extra strong shoes. The vet completely restocked my veterinary supplies, free of charge, and gave both horses a check-up. In spite of all our adventures between Santa Lucía and Coihaique, Hornero had benefited greatly from not carrying me. He had become slightly lame again a few kilometres before Coihaique, but that was only because he had cast a shoe, and I'd had no more nails left with which to put another one on. During the next few days, I got my camera mended, my tape-recorder checked. I even had my teeth filled.

The fourth of March, 1985, the day before we were due to leave, was a very bad day for Chile. The local radio announced that there had been an earthquake in central Chile, with Viña del Mar, San Antonio, Santiago, and San Fernando, the horses' home, affected. A hundred people had been killed, with hundreds more injured. Hospitals were turning out people to make room for the worst casualties. Desperately I tried to get a message through to the Claro Liras, but all telephone switchboards were jammed by anxious people trying to get news of relations up north. I spent a few anxious hours before I heard that nobody in San Fernando at least, had been badly hurt.

The next day I set off again. I was determined to ride south as fast as possible. Winter was on its way. Every day I managed to save now would make things easier later on. We crossed the fabulous El Salto waterfalls and passed through

167

the hamlet of El Blanco. Then we climbed the magnificent but lonely mountains past Vista Hermosa and the Face of the Indian, climbing down into the little port of Puerto Ibanéz just four days later. There the wind never seemed to stop and the horses and I had a rough crossing on the ferry *El Pilcherito* to Chile Chico and Mallín Grande on the other side of Lago General Carrera. Said to be the second largest lake in South America, it spans the border, half in Argentina, half in Chile. The ferry was crowded with prosperous cattlemen from the north. They were on their way south to buy stock from the southern farmers, who found it impossible to feed all their cattle through the winter and were forced to sell some off cheaply.

One of these gentlemen, down from Puerto Montt, took a great fancy to my tent, and offered me two more horses in exchange for it. Hornero and Jolgorio did not appear to think much of the idea. Neither, as I stood there being buffeted by the freezing Patagonian wind, did I.

After we had disembarked from the ferry our route took us through endless rose-bush thickets ablaze with hips to Puerto Guadal, then over a high mountain pass to the tiny settlement of Puerto Bertrand. From there I decided to leave the mountainous track which had cost the horses and me so much effort to climb and to try to make my way along the valley instead.

On 17 March, while somewhere up the curve of the globe Irishmen were celebrating St Patrick's Day, I was sitting on the banks of the River Baker, the fiercest, widest and coldest river in all Chile. In spite of the fact that the sky overhead was dark and overcast, the water was an extraordinary bright blue colour. All morning I had ridden along the banks of the river in the faith that if I just followed its course I would reach the town of Cochrane, my immediate destination. The trouble was that the river had had so many bends and branches, often seeming to double back on itself or split in two. It was as though it was deliberately trying to hide its true course.

168

Cochrane could not be far away now, I told myself. But I felt sure it must be the other side of the swirling blue water. The afternoon was closing in. Already it was much colder. Something had to be done soon, I realized, trying to screw up my courage. If we were to make it overland as far as Caleta Tortel, the horses and I would have to swim this river many times. We might as well start now. We had swum other rivers, of course, but these had been narrow and sluggish compared with the Baker, which was as wide as three motorways and seemed to move just as fast too.

Hornero and Jolgorio had not, I imagined, done much swimming during their former careers as darlings of the Chilean rodeo; certainly, faced with the Baker, they did not think much of the idea. The term 'horse-sense' is more than just a cliché.

I tried to remember the rules for swimming fast rivers. You have to swim up-current of the horse, otherwise he may be dragged on top of you. It is vital never to put a rope around a horse's neck to hold onto because he might put his foot through it while swimming and drown. What the rules didn't tell you was how to get the horses into the water in the first place. The river-bed here dropped straight from its banks, with no shelf at all, and already Hornero and Jolgorio were behaving in much the same way as they had the night I'd camped too close to the precipice. The other problem was my equipment. Jolgorio could not carry it while swimming. How could I get it across? And wouldn't everything be ruined even if I did?

At last I got up and made my way further downstream. There was a place here where the river splayed out into five fingers with rocks sticking up in between. One of these, grey and grim and almost phallic in shape, was not far out of reach. Using a rope from the shore to save me from being swept away, I managed to get out to this rock and to feed yet another rope around it. This way the horses would be subjected to a forward pull if I tugged from the shore, encouraging them to enter the water.

Would it work? I would soon find out. The next task was to lash together four stout logs, of which there were plenty lying around. Onto this makeshift raft, I tied my rucksacks and other gear, swathed in most of the fifty new heavy-duty polythene bags I had bought while in funds in Coihaique.

Then, with a quick prayer, I climbed onto Hornero and tried to ride him into the river, using my heels and many words of persuasion. At the same time I pulled hard on the rope. Suddenly the bank seemed more or less to give way under his hooves.

It was a maelstrom of water, ropes, my possessions, and the frantic threshing of Hornero's hooves. I did not worry too much about Jolgorio. Just concentrating on keeping Hornero under control took all my strength and attention. If I could just keep him going in the right direction, his friend would follow. I was right. Shortly afterwards there was a loud splash. The bank was so steep that the horses could not get out and had to swim.

Already the current was taking hold of us. I slipped off Hornero's back, as he seemed to be having trouble swimming with my weight, and simply held onto his tail. Using an old Indian trick I had read about, I splashed water in his face to keep him from turning round. No longer able to hold the rope from my raft, I tied it to his tail. This slowed the poor horse down so much that Jolgorio was soon swimming quite far ahead. Indeed Hornero was only making about one yard's progress across the river for every twelve or so that we were hurtled downstream.

I opened my eyes again as the sharp stones near the other side ripped my clothes. We were across! It hadn't been a textbook crossing, but at least we had made it. And I was proud of my raft, which had worked quite well. The polythene provided buoyancy and the wood stability. It was almost as though my possessions had been floated across in an air bladder. I dried the horses and myself in front of a hastily

170

lit campfire, blessing the cheap cigarette lighter I had bought in Coihaique. Matches would never have made it, I felt sure.

Just as I was saddling up the horses I became aware that I was being watched. A little old man had come up quite silently behind me. As nonchalantly as possible, I went on with my tasks, trying not to show how frightened I had been by the crossing.

'How much further to Cochrane?' I asked the old timer.

'Oh, it's back across the river,' he replied.

When he saw my expression he smiled gently. 'Do not worry,' he said. 'I have a canoe. I will take you and your packs and tow the horses on a line. Don't worry, it will be no trouble . . . '

And so it was that late that evening we arrived at Cochrane, the last town of the archipelago, the place where all roads and tracks south finally come to an end.

The spectacular mountains around the town were getting whiter each day, and the farmers were making their last visit before the snows imprisoned them in their farms for the winter. They went home leaving behind the cows and the children they had arrived with – the cows sold to buy flour, sugar, *mate* and other stores to see them through till spring, the children boarded out with townsfolk so that they could go to school. It was a warning that winter would soon be here, making my journey much harder.

I spent four days making hurried preparations for the next part of my journey. As in Antofagasta, the local people were very worried when they heard my plans. The journey from Cochrane to Caleta Tortel was virtually impossible by horse, they told me firmly. There were swamps, impassable rivers, mountains with few footholds. Local people travelling down to the little rocky port would take their horses only as far as Lago Vargas, about three days' ride from Cochrane, then continue by boat.

'By boat?' I saw a gleam of hope. After all, Hornero and Jolgorio were used to travelling on boats. I suggested this.

171

'Oh no,' they said. The boats are just small ones, no horse could be carried in one. The River Baker was almost as hard to navigate as the terrain on either side of it and the only large craft to try to get down it was the twice-yearly raft, sent by the authorities to collect cattle. One had just left, so there would not be another for at least six months. Even the local horse nurse advised me to sell the horses and travel on by canoe.

I felt trapped. I could not go back. I could not stay forever in Cochrane. I could not, it seemed, go on, for I would not leave my horses behind. Their importance to me was at once the strength and the weakness of the expedition. Poor Hornero, poor Jolgorio, I thought, stroking their velvety noses. Was I really justified in trying to get through when even the locals who knew the region advised me against it?

Yet once again the alternative to putting myself and the horses through an ordeal was to abandon the whole adventure. All the thousands of miles we had travelled would have been for nothing. There are no excuses for losers, even losers against great odds, in the book business. Somehow we had to get to Caleta Tortel before the next naval ship called there. The likelihood of fulfilling the prophecy in the last paragraph of my original proposal – 'The horses will get as far as the Chilean naval base of Puerto Williams, ninety miles north of Cape Horn; I will set up camp there leaving them in charge as I set off to land on the Horn itself' – still seemed remote, but I couldn't bring myself to give up.

The people of Cochrane listened sympathetically as I explained all this. 'Well, you can always take the easier route to Villa O'Higgins and then ride south via Argentina,' they suggested.

Argentina! When I die they will find the name of that country written in my heart, I thought.

'Well,' said Sergio the horse nurse, 'if you really are determined to go to Caleta Tortel, one of the local settlers will show you the first part of the way. After that we shall just have to pray.' 'At best,' he added, 'the journey should take you about twenty days.'

Twenty days! According to my map the distance was well under a hundred kilometres.

'Yes,' Sergio replied, 'but here the condors do not fly in a straight line!'

> 'No game was ever yet worth a rap,
> For a rational man to play,
> Into which no accident, no mishap,
> Could possibly find its way . . . '

This verse kept running through my head as I rode along on 22 March, the first morning out of Cochrane. I would have had more confidence in its sentiments if its author, Adam Lindsay Gordon, had not later shot himself in despair.

Chapter Sixteen

———— ✖ ————

Slowly, carefully, I led Jolgorio across the swaying wooden suspension bridge. It was of the type usually seen in Westerns. This one, however, was already long past the age of retirement. Many of the wooden slats and most of the handrail were missing. The bridge drooped down into a deep ravine between two high ledges. From somewhere below came the sound of crashing water, but all I could see was a tangled landslide of rocks and dead trees far beneath us.

I had spent more than an hour sitting looking at the bridge trying to screw up my courage to cross it. Telling myself that the settlers and their horses must use it and therefore so could we. One day out of Cochrane the realities of the present stage of my journey were already hitting me hard. The settlers probably looked upon this swaying contraption as a tremendous boon. Certainly if I really wanted to get my horses and myself to Caleta Tortel, there was simply no alternative but to cross it.

I had tried Hornero first, taking even his saddle off to save every extra ounce. The whole bridge had shuddered and swung from side to side at every step. Again and again we'd had to stop and wait till it settled down a bit. Those moments, as I'd stroked Hornero with hands clammy with sweat, reaching for the secret door to his trust which lay somewhere behind his ears, had seemed endless. Now at last he was safely on the other side and it was Jolgorio's turn.

All went well until Hornero gave an encouraging whinny

from the other side. Jolgorio tossed his head and gave an answering call, quickening his pace. Suddenly it seemed that not just the bridge, but the whole forest world far beneath us was swinging violently from side to side. Jolgorio seemed to lose his foothold and almost fell, his forehooves flailing desperately. All at once there was a loud crack and his off hind foot broke through one of the rotten wooden slats. All it needed was for him to panic and we would both plunge to our deaths a hundred feet below. Already the part of the bridge under us was disintegrating as he struggled, his eyes wide with fright.

'*Calma . . . calma . . . calma*,' I pleaded. I clung desperately to the horse, trying to soothe him. '*Calma*.' Then, very slowly, I bent down and with great difficulty extricated the hoof from between the planks. That small amount of hard-won trust had saved us. When we at last reached the other side, I collapsed on the wonderful firm ground. Thank God real fear only hits you after the danger is over, I thought. Then I realized I would have to make two more journeys to fetch the packs and the saddles.

The next crossings of the river were by the old method, and the Baker demanded a price every time we swam it. The currents would burst open my prematurely aged plastic bags, ruining or making off with one possession after another. We swam it again and again. Every few kilometres the terrain on one side of the Baker's banks would become impassable and the horses and I had to cross to the other and try our luck there. All this practice improved our swimming techniques. Hornero swam with his teeth showing. Jolgorio, being somewhat fatter, rolled a little from side to side, while I just tagged along, with Hornero kindly permitting me to hold onto his tail. When we weren't swimming we were plunging through swamps up to the horses' withers, leaping through undergrowth which seemed to have been untouched since the world began or climbing rocks. Here and there among the mountains I saw little splashes of red paint on the rocks, the

175

work of the surveyors preparing a route for the Carretera Austral.

In spite of having unlimited trees to nibble, the horses were badly missing good fodder. This made me feel guilty every time I opened my own carefully wrapped swag bag of bread and dried meat. However, as dusk fell on our third day out of Cochrane, I saw a wonderful little grassy island right in the middle of the river. We swam across and I set up camp and let the horses roam the island freely, eating their fill.

There followed a wild and stormy night with the rain lashing down. But I felt snug and secure in my tent, with all my strongest tentpegs out. My clothes were still wet from swimming the river, it was true, and as usual it had been quite impossible to dry them, but by now I was quite used to being wet. I could even put on wet socks in the morning without a shudder. No harm seemed to come of it. I was feeling rather smug. The real answer, I decided, was not to struggle against the odds to keep dry, but to become so accustomed to being wet that it no longer mattered.

I went to sleep feeling at peace with the world, the rain outside beating a lullaby on the canvas. All night I dreamt I was swimming. When I awoke I found to my horror that I *was* – or very nearly. The river had risen dramatically during the night. The island had almost disappeared. The horses stood close to the tent looking desolately at the swirling water all around them. What on earth were we to do? 'This is it!' I thought despairingly, 'I have made one mistake too many.'

There was no time for thought. Malevolent brown torrents were rushing by dangerously close to the tent. We could not stay where we were. Already most of the beautiful grass which had lured us across to the island had disappeared. Soon the entire campsite would be under water.

Frantically I packed everything away and loaded the raft. Thank God I had kept it. These rafts were usually very temporary affairs, just four logs lashed together on which to float my rucksacks. Because they were easy to make and too

176

heavy to take with us, I simply made a new one each time we had to cross the river. But this one I had kept, knowing I would need it to get back from the island. And this, of course, is exactly what I was going to have to do – but in very different circumstances from the previous day. The river had completely changed its character: its innocent bright blue colour, which had always enchanted me, had gone. It was now the colour of lead. The sky above was a sickening yellow, dotted with black clouds that looked so solid it seemed that were they to fall from the sky they would crush the whole world.

There was no time to be lost. I shouted at the poor terrified horses and whacked them on their rumps, aware I might be undoing months of painstakingly won trust. There was no other way to get them to go into the raging water. At last they lost their footing as the mud disintegrated underneath them and were swept away by the torrent. I plunged in after them, clinging desperately to the edge of the raft.

For once I had not had to screw up my courage. There had been no choice, no alternative. I looked back to where our island had been. It was gone. I could see the horses ahead of me, their heads appearing and disappearing in the waves. I prayed that, because of the river's many curves, bends and spits, we would be thrown onto one of its banks and not carried on downstream.

Huge tree roots and branches snatched by the river during its flooding were propelled along with us. As I clung on to the little raft, to my great delight the shore seemed to be coming closer. Then all at once a new current gripped me. Water was forced in through my nose and mouth and I felt I was being churned round and round in a washing machine. My head was roaring from trying to hold my breath. 'This cannot last forever,' I told myself. 'Even if I am drowning, it cannot last forever.' The rope with which I had tied myself to the raft was cutting into me. Somewhere in my mind I was aware that I was making no more effort, just hanging limp. If only the

177

roaring would stop.

Suddenly it had. I opened my eyes. I had arrived. The raft was caught in a thorn bush near the edge of the river. The sun was shining. The river was turning blue again and its level was falling. I pulled myself and the raft up the bank and very shakily got to my feet, hardly daring to look around me for the horses. When I did they were nowhere to be seen. I at once set off along the bank in search of them. A future without Hornero and Jolgorio was no future at all.

About a mile downriver I spied a large patch of white in the grass. It was Hornero, stretched out on the ground. I rushed forward, fearing the worst. But as I got closer he stirred and rolled over, then again, and again, his silver shoes flashing in the sun. I ran up to him and hugged him. He looked quite astonished. Not far away I found Jolgorio. He too seemed quite happy. He greeted me with a soft whicker and carried on eating. I felt almost mad with relief. Everything was all right, after all. They each had one or two minor scratches, but that was all. I cantered them briskly back to where my possessions were to check this, and to warm them up. Then I gave each of them a vitamin injection as a preventative measure. Hornero seemed to consider this the worst part of the whole escapade.

All my possessions were soaked through. Water sloshed around inside the camera. Soon the bushes around blossomed out in clothes and bits of saddlery spread out to dry. I blessed the warm sunshine. I blessed the river. I felt like yelling and shouting and singing for joy. As many times before on this expedition, I was astonished at how, far from leaving lingering despair or fear, an awful ordeal would bring exhilaration, even exaltation, afterwards. The only real casualty of the previous twenty-four hours was some of my film, which had been ruined when one of my plastic containers had burst open.

The sun was still high as we got under way again. After a short while I reached a fork in the trail. The two paths ahead

178

of me scarcely deserved the name. They were more like the indistinct paths of some rare wild animal, rarely trodden on and with no foot, paw or hoof marks visible – just the air of something at some time having been disturbed. As I stood trying to puzzle out which way to go, I thought I heard voices coming from beyond the right-hand fork's next bend. '*Adelante,*' I said to the horses and trotted off to investigate.

'*Hola gringa!*' a voice said.

It was Jorge Chodil, a Chilote Indian I had last seen in Cochrane five days before. The townsfolk had spoken of him as the uncrowned king of the River Baker. At the request of the mayor, he had shown me the route out of Cochrane, but he had seemed very arrogant and I had been glad when we had parted. Now he seemed much more friendly.

He was sitting beside a small campfire, sipping *mate*. He filled the *mate* up with more water from the kettle balanced on the fire and handed it to me.

'How have you got on?' he asked, his eyes twinkling. 'Any problems since Cochrane?' He looked just like a Leprechaun, with a mischievous face and snowy white hair sticking out from beneath a tattered sombrero.

'Oh no,' I lied, 'none at all. It's been quite easy . . . '

After a while he got up, stamped out the fire, and somehow climbed on top of his enormous shaggy horse. His stirrups reached only a few inches down either side of the horse's back, and the saddle itself was piled high with *pellones* or sheepskins. It looked as though he was perched on a sort of 'howdah' on top of the huge animal.

His other horse was carrying a very interesting packsaddle constructed out of handworked leather cords, plaited bamboo and many sheepskins in which was obviously ensconced a treasure of supplies and comforts for the winter. He saw me looking at it and told me his packhorse, being young and inexperienced, had fallen twenty feet down a rockface the day before. Not only had the horse been completely unhurt, but, he added proudly, the packsaddle and pack had stayed in

179

place and even his winter carafe of wine had remained unbroken!

He dug his heels into his horse's flanks and set off down the track at a furious pace with Hornero and Jolgório and I having to struggle to keep up. For the first time on the expedition they did not seem to resent the presence of other horses. In fact Jolgorio seemed delighted to be able to have a gossip with another packhorse.

At last we came out of the forest onto the river bank again. Señor Chodil slid off his horse and, cupping his hands, gave several loud whistles. A few minutes later, a red rowing-boat bumped against the bank, manned by his wife and son.

'What luxury,' I thought as Señor Chodil and I were rowed across the river, all possessions safely on board, the horses being towed on a line behind. At the other side nine of his children were waiting excitedly. I joined the long procession to his house.

It stood out bravely against glowering mountains which nobody would ever climb because behind these reigned the northern icecap. All around were tangled broken trees, evidence that here even the forest couldn't thrive. Yet close to the little wooden building was green grass, and a garden of wheat and cabbage and other vegetables. Also a carefully built corral containing about five cows and their half-grown calves.

Señor Chodil was well under five foot tall, but his spirit was a giant one. 'If you will the wish,' he said, 'then the means will follow.' He had run away from his home in Castro, Chiloé, when he had been just ten years old and had worked as a peon and a miner for more than thirty-five years before saving enough money to buy some cattle and put up a fence round a plot of land on the banks of the Baker. Now aged seventy-four, he had ten children aged between five and twenty-four. All but one, who was married, still lived in the tiny wooden house which he had built in 1944 with his own hands. 'I have no money,' he said, 'but I have all this.' He indicated his

180

family. 'Also I have my own meat, vegetables, endless firewood, endless water. And if this house does ever fall down I have plenty of wood and time to build another . . . '

One of the few things in the house which he had not made himself was the elegant iron stove, which was the pride of the family's tiny living-room and kitchen. He held an oil lamp closer so that I might see the writing. 'Sonnybridge, Dover, England' said letters clearly embossed on the metal. 'So you see it is a gringo stove,' he laughed. He had bought it off a ship which had called at Caleta Tortel and had towed it up here by raft.

This was my cue to ask him about the next stage of the journey.

'I can see that the bad animal of obstinacy is on your back – much as it used to be on mine,' he said. 'From here to Caleta Tortel will not be easy with the horses.' He leaned closer. 'As it happens I may be able to help.'

He explained that although the journey overland to Tortel was extremely hazardous, by rowing-boat it was fairly easy and only took two days, which was why his younger children were to go to Caleta Tortel for their winter schooling instead of to Cochrane. 'We shall be leaving in a few days,' he added, 'and can take your baggage. Without packs, your horses should be able to make it all right.' He and his wife would come along personally to supervise the operations and to arrange rendevous where I could meet up with them at night and have the use of my tent. The rest of the party would consist of the two young schoolboys and two older sons to help with the rowing. They all tried to hide the fact that by helping me their own journey would take longer, and that they would have to leave behind one or two of the bags of potatoes which they'd hoped to sell in Tortel.

Preparations were almost complete when suddenly the rains started again. Jorge's wife María Elina put aside the large bags of provisions she had prepared for the journey. That one should never leave one's house while it was raining

181

was one of the family's firmest rules. After my ordeal with the disappearing island, I knew they were right. The river had risen again, and the moodstone of its water colour was once more a treacherous muddy brown.

I tried to imagine that I was on a boat, lying ahull for better weather. But somehow it is much easier to accept that nature is boss when one is at sea. Meanwhile the Chodils said a tearful farewell to their cows, especially the favourites, Pampa, Coliflorita, and La Pata. I helped them milk the beasts one more time, ashamed that my wrists ached so, and that little Gina, just five years old, managed to get more milk out than I did! Then the animals were turned out to fend for themselves through the winter. Before they said goodbye to them, the Chodils hung leafy garlands around the cows' necks, then gave each a smart slap on the rump to see them on their way and to hide the affection they obviously had for them. Their horses, too, had their shoes taken off and were turned out into the mountains, the family having no further use for them till the following spring.

LOG: *1 April 1985 (April Fool's Day); House of Chodil*
The highest mountains all round have turned white overnight and thick frost is lying over the dome of my tent, making it look like a real igloo. The snows could fall at any time now, the Chodils tell me, making overland journeys impossible till next spring. However, although there is need for haste before this happens, we are still prisoners of the swollen river and yet again cannot leave today. Hornero and Jolgorio are very well and rested, but grass is getting very scarce.

Mr Chodil is sipping *mate* through a special *bombilla*, given to him forty years ago when he was working in the coal mines across the border in Argentina. Now he is wearing a pair of ancient glasses and reading aloud from a scroll of poetry which seems as endless as the river.

'There's a high road and a low road leading to the

182

same place,' he reads. 'From the high road you may see more – but also you may fall.'

Getting to know a little more about this family, who are even more extraordinary than the terrain they live in, is a very real recompense for being stuck here. In this household everything is shared. The *chicha* wine, having survived its fall with the horse, is passed around in one large cup from mouth to mouth, till all thirteen of us have had a calculated sip. The *mate* too is passed round – maybe also the germs, though I'm sure these are less contagious than the friendship passed with them. María Elina persists in beguiling me into the house for endless *mate*, meals, and warmth from the Sonnybridge stove – on the false promise that in return they will come out to my tent for a picnic before we leave.

Meeting her, I feel I've got to understand more about pioneering women all through history. She is a true mixture of velvet and steel. Sitting there in the soft candlelight, with her hair hanging down, she hardly looks more than a young girl herself, yet she has had ten children and has led a life most European women would think exceptionally hard. Many Chileans have an illusion about 'gringas' being liberated and independent. However, this woman, while adoring her husband, performs tasks most dedicated women's libbers would quail at. I find myself staring fascinated at her hands as she strums her guitar – hands which in the last two days I've seen wielding an axe, roping a sheep, milking a cow, pulling a rough oar. Can the delicate fingers playing gentle guitar music to put the youngest children to sleep really belong to the same hands which have done all this?

The children, if anything, are even more remarkable than their parents. The nine of them are crowded into this one small room with a sort of harmony and peacefulness which I think would be impossible for a European family in similar circumstances. Martin is carving an

183

animal out of a piece of wood. His brother Jorge is playing the mouth organ to accompany his mother. Little Gina, the youngest, is dancing delightedly in the new red shoes Mr Chodil had brought for her from Cochrane. Now that the cows have gone for the winter, and there is no more milk, she drinks only diluted *chicha* wine, being considered too young for *mate*, and becomes merrier all the time!

The rest of the children are sitting talking quietly to each other, or helping prepare the supper. It seems incredible that except for the two eldest, who have been to Cochrane, these children have never seen a road, or a car, or even a bicycle. They have known neither electric light, nor discos, nor television. They do not even have any neighbouring children to play with. Their only entertainment is an old radio . . . and each other. Yet they seem remarkably content.

I thought of the surveyors' red splashes which I had seen on the earliest part of my journey from Cochrane. What would happen when the government's promises were fulfilled and the road finally arrived here? Would things get better or worse for these people? What would happen when the first shiny jeeps full of tourists arrived at the River Baker?

At last two days later a starry night kept its promise and turned into a fine though bitterly cold morning. It was time to go. The Chodils showed me the way as far as the base of Cerro Negro. Then they said goodbye. 'Don't worry,' smiled María Elina, 'we'll have your tent up and waiting for you at the first rendezvous.' A little later as I climbed upwards I saw them set off down river, their little boat carefully packed to the gunwales. I felt a pang as I caught a glimpse of my green rucksack. I think I knew even then that I would not see the boat again that day.

Cerro Negro reminded me of a Dartmoor tor magnified

perhaps a hundred times. The rock steps and hollows were interspersed with soft green ledges. Some of these gave secure footing for the horses, others were slippery. There was no way of telling which type it was beforehand. Gradually I coaxed the horses upwards, knowing that to reach Tortel I had to get to the other side. At last, flanks heaving, covered with sweat, the horses stood on the top. So far so good, I thought, patting them. Going down the other side was even more difficult, with the firmest ground for hooves just inches away from a sheer fall. However, we had encountered quite a few of these types of descent on our journey from Cochrane and the horses had learnt simply to slide down the rocks, four hooves square and together.

At the bottom of the *cerro* we entered a part of the world where the forest looked as though it had not been touched for a thousand or more years. A green canopy spread a glow over everything, beautiful but deadly, because the lovely green moss carpet hid patches of dangerous swamp. I struggled along in front of the horses, not offering much by way of example because I kept falling every second step. My hair, my face, my clothes were soon covered in thick slime. Every now and again the tremendous effort of pulling their hind legs out of the thick goo would send one or other horse pitching forward onto his knees. It was absolutely terrifying. I cursed myself for bringing the horses here. As usual everyone's advice had proved correct. Why *had* I come? I also cursed the camera swinging round my neck, covered with mud. It seemed to mock the fact that my book would require photographs. It was almost as though this wild place was determined to remain secret forever, by making it impossible even to take a picture.

As I struggled on, hour after hour, I was far from alone. Large orange-breasted birds hopped around, so tame I had to shoo them away from the horses' legs. There were owls, and many butterflies. I also saw a large bird like a vulture, black with powerful white-tipped wings and a white collar round

185

his neck. He had a sort of bonnet in front of his strong curved beak, and it was only by this that I recognized him as a condor.

The swamp became worse as the trees thinned out again. By late afternoon we were struggling through terrible bogs with sharp spikes beneath the surface of the mud. The poor horses seemed to fall to their bellies every second step. At times there seemed no way forward at all, as one's feet groped blindly for solid ground and found none, only a deep hole. The poor horses were absolutely exhausted. Every now and then even Hornero would stand stock still, his eyes full of despair. The trouble was that I knew that to give up and go back would now be even more difficult than pressing forward. So I'd lift the horses' feet one by one and place them forward till they got going again. My great dread was that one of them might break a leg. If this did happen I had no gun or any other means of putting them out of their misery.

Very gradually, we got through the worst of the bog and entered an area of tall dead trees. By this time dusk was falling and it was quite clear that I would never get to my rendezvous with the Chodils. I regretted telling them not to worry about me. It was already much colder. Why had I allowed myself to get separated from my faithful tent and sleeping-bag? Yet if we had had to carry them, common sense told me, we would never have got through. Near a stream I found a tree with a hole near its root which I fancied might give good shelter. I decided to stop there for the night. I stripped the horses' headcollars off so they could relax better. I didn't think that after today's ordeal they would want to wander far. At least now I had an opportunity to wash the worst of the mud off. I felt inside the pockets of the old windcheater I was wearing under my poncho and got out the emergency box of matches I always carried. A fire would do a great deal to cheer up the situation. When I opened the box I found one match inside. It was damp.

There was nothing to do but wait till dawn. I cut a hole in

the horse blankets Hornero had been wearing under his saddle, and used them as additional ponchos; however, these were still damp and heavy with mud. Then I made a sort of burrow under the gaps in the roots of my tree, managing to grub out quite a good hole in the soft forest bed. I put on my sheepskin chaps which I always carried, curled up in a foetal position with the knees of the chaps up against my chin – and blessed the kind man from Coihaique who had given them to me. 'This,' I thought, 'has definitely been the hardest day of the whole expedition.' Then I stuck my head under the sheepskin off my saddle and tried to sleep.

It began to rain and water soon was dripping relentlessly from the branches of the trees. Drip, drip, drip, went the rain, splashing down on my neck. I shifted my position, but the drips followed me. When I did drift off to sleep, the rain and the cold would soon wake me. The horses seemed unhappy too, moving around me restlessly. From time to time Jolgorio would bend his head and shove me gently with his nose, as though to ask, 'Why haven't you arranged things better?'

Chapter Seventeen

———⬥———

I awoke at dawn, half conscious of the fact that inside the sheepskin chaps my legs were icy cold. Otherwise I felt quite comfortable and peaceful. If only my legs would stop bothering me. 'Stupid sheepskins,' I thought, suddenly irritable. Something was nagging away at the back of my mind. But it was hard to concentrate. My brain felt quite dull. I just wanted to relax.

But I couldn't. Not quite. So instead, after a while, with a great effort, I opened my eyes. To my surprise, the ground all around my hole was covered with frost crystals. Hornero and Jolgorio were standing close by, looking rather miserable, their breath thick steam. As I struggled to sit up, the damp horse blankets I had heaped on top of me the night before crackled.

At that moment I realized that large parts of my body had gone numb. The sheepskins had probably saved my life, keeping me just this side of hypothermia. My hollow had provided little protection, being much too shallow. Really, the humblest rabbit could have built a better hole. Clutching at the tree trunk for support I hauled myself to my feet. I would have given anything for a hot drink.

My hands looked like red lumps. I banged them together again and again, and stomped up and down my little glade. Gradually the day brightened, the first rays of chilly early morning sunlight creeping through the trees. Definitely, we were near the end of this dead forest. Also near the river. I was sure I could smell it.

I couldn't do the girths up tight as my hands were still very painful. It didn't matter. I would be walking anyway. Just then I noticed behind me, on the track we had already covered, a gap in the brush which I had not spotted the night before. Through it a trail of frozen mud led steeply downwards. It took a lot of effort to coax the reluctant horses through. They were losing faith in me – and after yesterday, who could blame them?

But all at once I felt I ought to be vindicated in their eyes. We emerged onto a lovely grassy bank, beyond which, wide and placid at this point, flowed my friend the River Baker.

Presently I heard shouts. Completely forgetting I had not tightened Hornero's girths, I leapt on top of him and galloped forward. Moments later the Chodils were standing around me laughing. I was still in the saddle, it was true, but it had slipped round so far that I was almost peering up from in between Hornero's front legs.

My friends had been very worried and had moved their camp several times the previous day, thinking I must have gone further than I had planned. This indeed was so, as it turned out. We were now, they told me, only about nine kilometres from Caleta Tortel. I had almost got through.

Not far off, like a fantasy come true, María Elina, still clad in her very best travelling overcoat, more suitable really for a visit to the shops than for a journey down river in the wilderness, was stirring a pot on top of a beautiful blazing fire. The two younger children were still asleep, under a rough shelter of polythene and pieces of wood. My tent, unused, stood waiting for me. 'Why didn't you borrow it?' I asked. 'We always camp this way when on a journey,' Jorge Chodil explained. 'It is our custom.' I thought of the fierce frost in the night. But everything here looked well organized and cosy; the wonderful heat from the fire was the secret, spreading everywhere. My tent, in which my belongings had been put, was by comparison damp. María Elina very

189

discreetly encouraged me to remove all my clothes, wrapping me in her husband's poncho. Then she hung my clothes up to dry. The older sons went off and chopped more wood, arranging it neatly near the fire in a series of 'Eeyore' houses, straight out of *Winnie the Pooh*.

After breakfast, the Chodils packed everything back into the little red boat and took me across the river, towing my horses behind. At the other side, young Jorge, the Chodils' eldest son, offered to accompany me, riding Jolgorio. He could show me the way. The horses seemed to consider this a good opportunity for a race and neither of us could hold them in as they galloped nose to nose at breakneck speed through the easy going at the other side of the river. They were so full of beans, it seemed incredible that only the day before I had worried that their hearts might give out. Now I marvelled at them as they accelerated; Hornero, under me, felt like a racehorse. Jolgorio, too, was at full stretch. Young Jorge crouched low on his back, seeming almost part of him. Once again, I nearly cried aloud in pure joy.

By midday, the easy going of the grassy bank had come to an end, our route evolving into a muddy track strewn with large tree trunks. Sometimes there were two – or even more – trees in a row and the horses had to jump them, taking off from deep mud, landing in more mud on the other side and then, within just a stride or two, taking off again. Neither of my horses had done much jumping before. As with polo ponies, it is a skill not taught as part of their extensive education.

Hornero seemed capable of raising himself on his hind legs then catapulting himself up into the air from a virtual standstill with a movement that reminded me of his Spanish Riding School cousins. He seemed to love jumping. Jolgorio, on the other hand, launched himself at each obstacle with an almost audible groan. Sometimes he made bad mistakes and got his legs caught up in branches which threatened to bring him down. He kept going, though, always somehow gamely

190

arriving on the other side. When he thought he couldn't jump, he'd scramble over.

At last we arrived at Punta Canela, just two kilometres from Caleta Tortel. Here we rejoined the Chodils. They had pulled up their boat, and were talking to an old man outside a tumbledown wooden hut. Filling most of the inside of the hut was an enormous black sow and her family of five contented snoozing piglets and one squealing unhappy one, which the old man was trying to sew into a sack, apparently in order to take it to Caleta Tortel in his own small rowing boat.

'You'll find no place to keep the horses in Tortel,' he warned me. 'It's just a rock. That is why I keep my pigs here. Why don't you leave them here to rest for a few days, while you make plans,' he added. 'There's plenty of good pasture on the banks around my hut.'

I took advantage of the old man's generous offer and turned them loose. Jolgorio, always the most articulate of the two, gave a loud whinny of pleasure as both horses began cropping the succulent-looking grass. In *The Voyage of the Beagle* Darwin had written: 'The traveller . . . will discover how many truly kind hearted people there are with whom he never before had, or ever again will have, any further communication, who are yet ready to offer him the most disinterested assistance . . . ' My journey was proving over and over again that this still was so.

Mists rolled down from rocky mountains rising sheer from the water as the Chodils' boat made its way steadily downstream towards Caleta Tortel. Ahead of us the river split into many branches, interspersed with swampy islands. All at once the little boat had quite a different feel about it. I think I knew before I dipped my finger in the icy water and tasted it salty that at last we had reached the end of the great River Baker and were on the level of the great channels reaching out from the mazes of uninhabited islands to the sea.

We moored the little boat off what looked like a small airstrip and I followed the Chodils over nearly a mile of slippery log pontoons across yet another swamp. This ended abruptly at a huge rock with another strip of pontoons leading over it. Half an hour later I was standing on a high ridge looking down onto twin coves on the other side. I had arrived in Caleta Tortel. Along the nearside of the two small coves was a row of rickety wooden houses, most with polythene flapping in their windows instead of glass. Their backs clutched at bare rock or straddled patches of bog. Their fronts stood braced against collapse by stilts sticking down into the sea. The houses were connected by yet more pontoons, again with legs sticking down into the water. They ran all around the shoreline. Behind the houses some scrubby trees gave here and there some pretence of green, but underneath these, clearly visible even from a distance, was just more rock and bog. It seemed a very strange place indeed.

The whole of the tiny settlement was a network of wooden steps, pontoons and scaffolding. There were no natural paths at all; indeed there was hardly enough level ground to pitch a small tent on. It was the very first place in Chile where I saw no gardens growing vegetables, no sheep or cattle or domesticated animals. Nothing but bare houses clinging to bare rock.

Towards the far end of the further bay the houses seemed rather newer and more securely built, painted white or blue instead of being just bare damp-looking wood, and there were some offices. Steps led up to a large yellow building which proclaimed itself School F 48 Caleta Tortel. Further on stood some prefabricated aluminium builings glinting silver in the weak sunlight, and hinting of government or naval subsidy. Never had I seen such a desolate and totally artificial place. Life here must be very hard indeed, I thought. The only excuse for Caleta Tortel's existence was the very reason I had struggled so hard to get there – namely that from time to time naval ships called in on their way southward through the channels.

The Chodils had by now delivered their two younger boys

Friends along the way: *above*, the Chodil family; *below*, El Aysenino Porfiado.

Jolgorio is winched off the ferry at Puerto Williams.

into the care of their married daughter who lived in Tortel, and were eager to be off back upriver to their farm. It would take at least four days of strenuous rowing. Saying goodbye was difficult. Señor Chodil's protective shield of arrogance was back in place. Our farewells were more formal than I would have wished.

A sign pointed to the offices of the *Alcalde del Mar* or Mayor of the Sea. In the north and in central Chile, there had been the carabineros. In the rain forest, building the new road, the military. But from here south, through a thousand desolate islands to Cape Horn itself, the *Armada*, the Chilean Navy, ruled supreme. A plump naval sergeant tapped a morse message through to Punta Arenas on my behalf. No, he didn't have information as to when the next ship would call, but would keep me informed.

As I left the *Alcalde del Mar's* office and made my way back along the slippery pontoon towards the other side of Caleta Tortel, where I had left my equipment, a man stepped briskly out of one of the wooden houses on the waterfront and blocked my path.

'Where are you going?' he enquired pleasantly. '*Soy Alejandro el Aysenino Porfiado*. I am Alexander the Obstinate One from Aysén.' Gleaming eyes peered from under an expensive but battered-looking sombrero. Shoulder-length hair and an unkept beard appeared necessary in order to give at least some privacy to an extraordinarily expressive face.

'Come with me,' he ordered, and steered me up some side steps and in through a crooked wooden doorway. Inside an exceptionally pretty dark-haired girl was stirring what looked like a fish casserole on top of a huge smoky stove. '*Aquí está Paola mi Señora*,' he said, introducing me to his wife. She smiled shyly and handed me a full plate.

'This', he announced, 'is your house, and here,' he pointed to an alcove, 'is your bedroom. There is no place for a tent in Caleta Tortel. Now we must collect your things and tomorrow we shall move your horses to a better place nearer Tortel

193

where there is plenty of grass. Meanwhile I shall prepare some warm water in a basin so you can soak your feet.' He seized a blackened kettle off the hob.

I'd had wet feet for weeks, and since it had seldom been possible to dry my clothes overnight, I had got quite used to putting on wet socks in the morning without a shudder. But now, peeling them off in front of my new benefactors was embarrassing. The wool socks seemed twice their normal weight, being laden with embedded bits of leaves and bog, and my feet were as white as those of a corpse, the chronically wrinkled skin on my toes giving the impression of their being webbed. The wonderful warm water seemed to seep right through to the bones, giving comfort that bordered an ecstasy. 'I understand,' my strange new friend said, looking amused. 'I understand your feet. You see, many of our paths have been the same, even if our dreams have been different.'

From time to time on my journey people had spoken of a flamboyant poet and musician walking and riding down Chile giving concerts. Now as I sat there in the small smoky room with my feet soaking in the basin, I realized I had just met him. He explained that some years before, having been inspired by the hard pioneering life of the settlers in his native region of Aysén, he had decided to travel through the whole of Chile by primitive means. He had spent the past five years walking and riding through his country. Now he was busy building a *chalupa*, a traditional sailing boat of the type I had seen constructed in Chiloé; he planned to sail it down through the islands to Puerto Natales.

El Aysenino understood my obsession about always putting my horses first; he told me that the greatest tragedy of his journey had not been when he had nearly cut off his own right hand with an axe, but when two of his ten horses had died. One from colic. The other from the fate poor Jolgorio had so narrowly escaped – being eaten by hungry settlers. His most recent tragedy had been when his dog had drowned in the River Baker after becoming impaled on one of the deadly

194

sharp spikes my horses and I had been so lucky to avoid.

Next day he helped me get Hornero and Jolgorio from Punta Canela to a little island across the bay from Tortel where there was plenty of good grass and where they could stay safely till the ship came.

LOG: *7 April 1985; Caleta Tortel*
Easter Sunday. Never have I felt further away from the spring daffodils of Wales. Instead, here in the far Southern Hemisphere winter is approaching fast and it looks as though I may be seeing Cape Horn in its thick snowy coat – a sight not many yachtsmen can afford. The *Alcalde del Mar* says I may have to wait quite a while for the next naval ship to call. The good news is that a kindly admiral in Punta Arenas has radioed permission for the horses and I to be given passage when it does.

So, I still cannot say how much longer this journey will take. Hard as I try to wrest the helm of decision away, fate and the weather, twin captains of this expedition, snatch it back.

In the end I had to wait in Caleta Tortel for nearly a month and I grew to hate the place. No doubt this was partly because I felt trapped. For once I could not simply saddle up and go. I was utterly dependent on the kindness of the *Armada*. It wasn't a good feeling. However, I also felt depressed by the all-pervading atmosphere of discontent that hung over the tiny settlement. It was the first place I had seen in Chile where many people really seemed to be unhappy. At first it seemed that their troubles were caused by nature's own miserliness. Here there was no land where families could grow their own vegetables, or keep chickens or a sheep or pig. Maybe this was why the pride and independence I had seen among the poorest people during my journey through Chile did not exist here.

When I asked El Aysenino Porfiado about it, his cheery

195

manner vanished immediately. 'The fault', he said bitterly, 'is not nature's, nor the *Armada's*. It lies at the door of the Municipalidad Civil which arrived here in 1982. Before that people led hard lives and were poor, but they were much happier. They were free, you see . . . ' He described how men would go off for weeks in their little rowing boats, equipped with a few essentials and a crude axe, in order to cut trees on one of the uninhabited islands, to get the hardwood beams that were highly valued in central Chile. Eventually they'd row back to Caleta Tortel towing great rafts of beams lashed together to sell to the next naval vessel in exchange for supplies. It was hard, brutal work, but they were proud of it and managed to keep their families well. However, as soon as the Municipalidad had arrived everything had changed. The wood was still shipped by the naval vessels, but first the settlers had to sell it to the municipal authorities, who set very high quotas to be met in return for the same basic minimum monthly wage of a Santiago streetsweeper – about 5000 pesos or £45 a month. Worst of all was that the people now had to buy what they needed at the expensive new supply depot the authorities had opened. 'It's slave labour,' El Aysenino snorted. 'The families can no longer manage,' he said, 'and people are unhappy. The trouble is that here we are so far from anywhere, the authorities think they can do what they like.' He gave me a hard stare. 'You, gringa, have a voice. If you care about Chile even a little, write about this when you get home.'

But was what he was telling me his opinion or was it fact? I could by now speak superficial Spanish fairly well. But I felt frustrated almost beyond endurance by not being able to converse adequately with this man. Night after night in his smoky little kitchen he asked endless questions about England, and in return told me stories of his five-year adventure which made my expedition seem a pleasure trip by comparison. Sometimes he would throw out challenging questions: how good were my horses really? Or did I think the

196

journey had been more difficult or easier because I was a woman? How did I feel? What was in my heart? What was in my head? Sometimes I felt like screaming, and our discussions would often end in arguments – and how can you possibly win an argument when you can't even speak the language properly? *'Hola gringa,'* he would say, smiling at Paola, 'you are *porfiada* (obstinate) like me.' Then he'd get out his guitar and sing a song he had composed about Hornero and Jolgorio and for a while peace would reign in the little household.

Gradually, as the days passed, more and more rowing boats came in, towing the huge rafts of handcut hardwood beams and poles for shipment to Punta Arenas. The timber piled up in giant towers on all the pontoons and jetties, higher sometimes than the surrounding houses. Excitement, too, was building up.

At long last, on 5 May, *barcaza* LSM *Elicura*, the naval supply ship, slid like a grey shadow into the bay and anchored, uttering several blasts on her horn. Later that day she came in stern first against the quay so that the timber could be loaded. She also made a brief visit to a neighbouring island to pick up more wood. The whole population of Caleta Tortel was suddenly seized by a frenzy of activity, carrying wood and other bits of cargo on board. Finally, on 7 May, it was time for the few passengers to board. Last of all came the horses, who by now I had brought over from their island retreat. Slipping and stumbling on the lethal pontoons, they made their way gamely forward, eventually leaping up the iron ramp of the boat like seasoned travellers. Minutes later they were snug on deep sawdust, in the special stalls which the crew had partitioned off for them in the hold.

Night fell as the *Elicura* steamed away towards Canal Mesier. The gentle lights of Caleta Tortel dimmed and then disappeared. I felt almost wild with excitement, totally intoxicated by the movement of the boat under me and the evocative smell of diesel from her engines – but most of all by the

197

wonderful feeling that at last we were on our way again. The horses when I checked them seemed quite happy, stripping leaves from the branches of bamboo I had brought for them to eat on the journey. The Captain had also brought several bales of hay from Punta Arenas as an emergency larder.

Comandante Roberto Veira Frías' thoughtfulness did not stop with the horses. Speaking excellent English, he told me that – in the absence of any accommodation for single women – he'd had a bunk prepared for me in the ship's small armoury. I could use the officers' showers and facilities and to eat with them in the wardroom. 'For the five days of this voyage,' he said, 'you must forget you are on an adventure and pretend you are on holiday!'

When I looked at my face in the shower-room mirror I had a shock. It was completely grey, with streaks of ingrained smoke from a hundred campfires. My hair was a sort of dirty dun colour, and stuck out in all directions. Now that I had time to study them properly, I could see that my hands were the worst of all, with deep chaps embedded with black. The dirt was deeply ingrained and did not seem to want to wash out no matter how much I scrubbed my hands in the new luxury of hot water. The backs were covered in half-healed cuts and scratches, with scabs which looked like the result of some dreadful skin disease. I felt ashamed – and even more appreciative of the Captain's kindness. At supper I ate my food trying to hid my hands under the table as much as I could, while the *Elicura*'s officers pretended not to notice and did everything possible to make me feel at home.

LOG: *9 May 1985; on board* LSM *Elicura*
Chunks of ice in the sea as the *Elicura* sails on past endless fjords, inlets and deeply forested mountainous islands rising steep from the water. These are uninhabited, experts say, even by wildlife, because they are so inhospitable. Their only contribution to the solid world is to stretch in a tortured maze between here and

198

the Southern Ocean.

All that the human race has ever been able to do with places like this is simply to give them names and then leave them alone. We're passing Little Wellington, Isla Middleton, Isla Swett. Then there's Peninsula Puckel, Thorton, the island of Middle, Islas Boxer and Williams, Islets Maud and Eva, named after statesmen and half-forgotten sailors, and the wives and sweethearts they never came back to.

Over the next two days we also passed Puerto Eden with its tiny settlement of indigenous Indians, Angostura Inglesa, El Paso del Indio, Canal Pitt, Canal Uribe. Then it was south through more open sea and the aptly named Bay of Troubles, to the fringes of the Southern Ocean itself. It had suddenly become much rougher. Waves started to break over the boat, some crashing in through gaps in the tarpaulin covering the hold, to drench the poor horses. Indeed, though the pumps kept working, they were sometimes standing almost up to their knees in water. They were by now real old salts, however, and had learnt to eat while balancing with their legs spread wide apart and swaying to counteract the surging of the boat. They seemed fine and never in any serious distress.

In spite of this rough weather towards the end, the voyage was indeed a 'holiday' for me as the Captain had promised. I was thoroughly spoilt and the *Elicura* was a happy ship and as full of character as her crew.

On 12 May the *Elicura* anchored off Isla Desolación to tend to Felix Lighthouse, the last of the many lights and buoys she had stopped to service en route. Then she turned to port. At long last we were sailing up the Magellan Strait, past breathtakingly beautiful ice-covered mountains on the left, and with the harsh brown outline of Isla Desolación still on the right.

On the next day, exactly nine months after my arrival in South America, the little supply ship docked in Punta Arenas and the horses and I disembarked. I gazed in amazement at the rushing cars and lorries on the busy shoreside road, astounded too by how many people there were and by the first stone houses I had seen for months. They seemed colossal. Soon two men dressed in the familiar green uniform of the carabineros arrived, together with some journalists. The horses and I shook hands and hooves for the cameras, at the request of a sentimental lady journalist. Then they were whisked off to comfortable stables and I to the hospitality house of the carabineros.

Punta Arenas seemed to be an interesting old city, but at that moment I was too bemused to take it all in. One thing in particular seemed very strange. 'Where,' I asked, 'is the famous Patagonian wind?' It is supposed to blow there continually and to be so fierce that the people have to cling to telegraph poles to stay upright.

'Oh that,' came the reply. 'The wind only blows in the summer.'

I went to sleep early in my comfortable bed, but kept waking up in the night. I felt deaf without the sound of the sea, or the forest, or the rushing River Baker, and numb without the cold night air on my skin.

In the days that followed I made plans for the next stage of the journey and sorted out my affairs. It was quite disturbing how easy everything was. I could at last get a message to England, by means of a simple telex, which arrived as I sent it. I was able to buy new batteries instead of heating up the old ones again and again. To purchase a litre of milk instead of having to milk a half-wild cow. To turn on a gas fire or plug in an electric kettle for coffee, instead of taking bits of wood to bed with me in my sleeping-bag, in an attempt to dry them for the next morning's campfire.

Chapter Eighteen

On our arrival in Punta Arenas Hornero had stolen the hearts of everyone. There had even been a photo in the local press showing me sitting under his stomach; the caption read: 'How the gringa sheltered from the rain!' However, it was fat little Jolgorio, a dark horse in more ways than one, who became the hero of Isla Navarino when the ferry took us there, five days later. He allowed himself to be winched off the boat in a sort of net. Then while Hornero, who had viewed attempts for the same to be done to him with complete horror, stayed on board, Jolgorio trudged through the snowy streets of the Chilean naval base of Puerto Williams flying the Union Jack from his bridle. He ended up outside the officers' quarters, where he was introduced to a distinguished naval commander with bushy eyebrows and much gold braid, and tried to drink his whisky.

'Chilean whisky?' I asked, remembering that in my original book proposal I had half jokingly promised to find out what they drank in the far south to keep out the cold.

'Oh no!' he replied. 'The best Ballantine's – all the way from Scotland!'

It was the final triumph, or nearly. I was almost at the end of my quest. There were only ninety more miles to go and I would be standing on the 1400-foot-high rock that was my destination – Cape Horn itself.

However, I soon found out that, like all my plans on this journey, to land on Cape Horn island in mid-winter would be difficult, if not downright impossible. The only boats which went out there in winter were occasional naval vessels to tend to the needs of the three lighthousemen who looked after the Cape Horn light and lived there all year round. The next of these ships would not be setting sail from Puerto Williams for at least five weeks. My spirits sank.

I stepped out of the warmth of the naval offices to be absorbed back immediately into the violent magnificence of the Magellanic climate. A gale was blowing the snow in almost solid horizontal sheets. Poor Jolgorio stood with drifts up to his stomach and with ice stiffening the whiskers at the ends of his nostrils. Behind the neat little yellow houses, the high mountain range known as 'Navarino's Teeth', white and gleaming with ice just an hour before, had now completely disappeared. Jolgorio looked very miserable. He was lonely and there was nothing for him to eat. It was clear he wanted to rejoin his friend Hornero, and go back to the stables in Punta Arenas.

His idea was a good one. After nearly ten months on the hoof, the horses' part in the adventure was nearly over. It would have been unnecessary hardship to have kept them in Puerto Williams for five weeks. I decided to return to Punta Arenas and then to ride north to Puerto Natales, where the horses could stay in far better conditions, while I came back to Puerto Williams alone to wait for my chance to get out to Cape Horn. Afterwards they'd be well positioned for the long journey home, as I'd heard that a boat ran from Puerto Natales up to Puerto Montt.

We arrived back in Punta Arenas on 21 May, national Navy Day. People were singing and cheering in the streets, smart naval officers were walking even taller than usual and Chilean flags flew from almost every house in town. It was the anniversary of the Battle of Iquique in 1879 when the old corvette *Esmeralda*, under the command of Captain Arturo Prat, had engaged in a seafight against great odds with her Peruvian enemy. She had fired her last cannon while two-thirds under water and then had gone to the bottom; the last thing visible was the Chilean flag still flying from her highest mast. Captain Prat and most of his crew had lost their lives, but their heroism has never been forgotten by the Chileans.

For the first time on my journey I set off northwards – to Puerto Natales. I was seen off by a distinguished-looking woman called Margot Duvalde, who as a shy eighteen-year-old girl had come to England to fly Spitfires in the Air Transport Auxiliary during the Second World War. She had recently retired from the Chilean Air Force.

The journey to Puerto Natales was also the first we had made in real southern weather. The horses and I were constantly caught up in blizzards so thick one could not see through them. Hornero and Jolgorio had to use the same technique for snowdrifts as those they had once discovered useful for dealing with deep sand in the Atacama. Occasionally, as I made my way through Villa Tehuelche, Morro Chico and Rubens, the sky would clear. Then I would gaze amazed at the plains stretching all the way to the horizon, inhabited by Hereford cattle, sheep and ostriches. The vastness of the great lonely estancias is necessary, it was explained to me, because in Patagonia it takes three acres to feed just one sheep. During winter the animals have to learn how to dig for their food. I physically had to demonstrate this to a puzzled Hornero and Jolgorio who'd never had to cope with such deep snow in their life before. I also had to introduce them to the art of breaking the ice on their drinking water.

Kindly people living in Punta Arenas had given me firm instructions to call at their isolated country estancias, where the staff looking after them made us very welcome and dished out huge amounts of stew for me and hay for the horses. The only owner I found actually braving the conditions to live at his farm in the winter was Maurice Castro, a young friend of Margot Duvalde's who bred black Aberdeen Angus cattle which any Scotsman would have been proud of. Sometimes the blizzards were so bad that I could see nothing at all. Then it was possible to locate the direction of an estancia house only by following the 'homing beacon' of its barking dogs.

As we neared Puerto Natales, the sky suddenly cleared and the sun came out. Snow flew from under the horses' hooves as they galloped along, neck to neck. At last, after ten months on the trail, I was so well organized that I could gallop even with the packs fully loaded without anything being shaken out of place, and could control both horses with my voice and one rein between the two of them. Suddenly I felt very sad. Just as I was beginning to really learn how to manage things on this expedition, it was ending. From now on the journey would be mostly in boats. This was the last week with Hornero and Jolgorio. The last time 'The Three Musketeers', as the Chileans had come to call us, would be on the trail together. An era was ending for us.

At Puerto Natales, the carabineros were waiting to care for the horses in their fine stables. The next day, a de Havilland Twin Otter arrived to fly me back to Punta Arenas, courtesy of the Air Force, though I suspected the influence of Margot Duvalde. Certainly I was being thoroughly spoilt.

Looking down on the Magellan Strait, I was surprised to find that it did not run in a straight line east to west, but in a pronounced V. Tierra del Fuego was a flat landscape of icy lakes, snow and blood red patches, which on closer inspection seemed to be some sort of mossy bog. It took me over a week to get from Punta Arenas to Puerto Natales, but only forty minutes to fly back!

Within a week I was back on Isla Navarino, having been given special permission to camp in what was normally a tight security area. For the first time for nearly twelve years I found myself battling with canvas in the Roaring Forties, even though this time it was only a tent – which quickly turned itself into a real igloo covered with ice and frost, my home, as it was to turn out, for more than three weeks.

I'm typing this almost horizontal, curled up in my sleeping-bag. These days, the sleeping-bag is the centre of my world. For outside my tent is thick white frost with every blade of grass sprouting a hundred fern fringes and the temperature is many degrees below zero. I go to sleep wearing two pairs of socks, as well as gloves and my navy-blue thermal balaclava. This must be even more off-putting than the traditional curlers and cold cream, so it is lucky there is nobody around to see me.

There are great rewards for all this though. In the mornings, after I have managed to prise the ice off the zip of the tent door, I can drink early-morning coffee in bed, watching the low winter sun rising just above the glaciers on the other side of the Beagle Channel, turning all the ice first to rare and beautiful shades of gold and red, then to a pink which seems to envelop my whole visible world. It is as though real country colours such as green and brown are not allowed here, and only the fantastic permitted . . .

Over the next two weeks the navigational chart I had bought in Punta Arenas came to life as Comandante Echeverría, chief of the naval base, gave permission for me to travel on board a small tug-like vessel called the *Fuentealba* when it made visits to various islands and places in the region. I made three trips on the *Fuentealba*, standing on the bridge as it threaded its way through the narrow channels between hundreds of deserted, desolate islands. It took me to Puerto Torro where I left my mark in the record book of the southernmost police station in the world; to Isla Picton, named after a famous Indian warrior. Another journey led through the narrow Murray Channel to Ponsonby Sound, named after one of the intrepid ancestors of my grandmother Cara Ponsonby. A little further on lay Milne Edwards and Button Islands. It was hard to take in the extraordinary desolation. Around me were more uninhabited islands than any schoolboy ever dreamed of.

On 27 June we sailed through the night to arrive at dawn at a beautiful inlet on Península Hardy called Orange Bay or Bahía Orange, an irridescent marmalade sky confirming its name as we anchored. The *Fuentealba*'s rubber tender landed with difficulty and I bent against a fierce south-westerly wind to climb up through contorted dwarf beech trees and tangled tussock grass to a high point where a plaque commemorated the fact that during the nineteenth century there had been a missionary settlement there.

Red rust now bit deeply into the roofs of the missionaries' ruined homes. A young lieutenant from my boat told me the sad tale of how they had killed their converts with kindness. For thousands of years the Yamana Indians had lived happily amid the maze of wild inlets and islands of the far south, travelling from place to place, tying their boats to the kelp and sending their women diving naked for the shellfish on which they subsisted. They had survived where no other race would even try. But the missionaries had introduced them to bread, which they were not used to, and to clothes which they did not know how to keep dry. Many had succumbed to disease. The result was that in the first hundred years from the missionaries' arrival the Yamanas' numbers had been reduced from four thousand to just twenty. Now no mammals, human or animal, live on Isla Hoste, the large island of which the peninsula is a part. No sheep nibble the thick tussock grass. It is simply too difficult to bring them there. For the same reason neither fox, nor rabbit, nor rat has ever arrived. Wildlife is restricted to that which has wings – condors, albatrosses and a variety of other seabirds.

Back in Puerto Williams I constantly plagued the Comandante with one question: when would a boat be going out to Cape Horn? He'd always smile politely and reply, 'Just a little longer. Have patience.' Then one day, the *Armada*'s attitude towards me seemed to change. I was on my way into

Puerto Williams from my campsite to do some shopping, when Comandante Echeverria's smart young aide came running up behind me.

'The Comandante wishes to see you at once,' he said.

My insides clenched with excitement. 'At last,' I thought. 'He's arranged for me to go to Cape Horn.' I was sure of it.

'I'm sorry,' he said as I entered his office. 'The Chilean Navy will never take you to Cape Horn.' All visits to Cape Horn from then on were to form part of a military operation on which civilians were not allowed. He told me that a naval plane would be leaving Puerto Williams the following morning and that I had better be on it.

I turned away, trying to hide my despair and disappointment. I had come so far, only to fail in my objective. Three thousand miles of riding and walking had been for nothing. All Hornero's and Jolgorio's efforts had been for nothing, so too the efforts of the hundreds of Chileans who had helped me on my journey.

Cape Horn had been my dream and my goal while I had sat beside my log fire in Wales planning the expedition. Cape Horn had still been my goal as I had struggled through sandstorms in the Atacama, snowstorms recently on the way to Puerto Natales, and swamps up to the horses' withers in the region of Aysén. Always the thought that I was on an odyssey back to Cape Horn had kept me going. But Chile is a land where authority means something, and this man's authority could stop me now as the weather never had my boat in 1973.

I had no catamaran *Anneliese* now. I was dependent on other people. The weight of the faith the publishers and a few other people had had in me to complete my journey successfully was something which little Jolgorio had never been able to carry, only I. Now I felt it more heavily than ever. The more I tried to explain in my bad Spanish, the less the Comandante understood.

'We cannot take everyone to Cape Horn who wants to go,'

he said, forgetting that previously he had promised to arrange it.

What had I done? Had I offended the *Armada* in some way?

Snow was still falling as I boarded the navy plane for Punta Arenas next morning, but the coldness I felt inside me had nothing to do with the weather.

'You realize they are entertaining the Argentinian admirals on Isla Navarino this weekend?' Bill Matheson, the British Consul, told me when I arrived in his office in Punta Arenas. He explained that, although the calibre of the Chilean *Armada* was very high, they were not a large nor rich navy, whereas the Argentinians were. The real reason for my sudden dismissal from Isla Navarino was suddenly obvious, and I couldn't blame the Chileans. Their relationship with Argentina was important and this was definitely not the moment to be entertaining an English gringa.

I recalled the Comandante's last words to me, when he had finally understood the extent of my disappointment.

'Don't worry,' he had said quite kindly. 'If you really want to get to Cape Horn you will get there. You will be back.'

I had to find a way!

A promise kept – back at Hacienda Los Lingues:
above, with Germán Claro Lira and his wife Marie Elena;
below, honoured guests at dinner.

A long way from home in Antarctica.

Odyssey achieved – at Cape Horn, 3 September 1985.

Chapter Nineteen

My friends in Punta Arenas were probably quite right. After they heard of the Comandante's decision, one after another they told me that Cape Horn was just a lonely, windswept, treeless island at the bottom of the world, no different, except for its unique geographical position, from a thousand other small islands in the region. It was not particularly beautiful or interesting and certainly didn't compare with other Chilean splendours I had passed through on my journey. But somehow their words didn't convince. For me, Cape Horn had always been the goal of my so-called odyssey on this continent. It was the point of the journey and, more important, the point of the book I hoped to write.

I devised a plan. I would get the horses safely home to the hacienda and then ask special permission from the government in Santiago to visit Cape Horn. If I succeeded it would be only an hour's flight from Santiago to the south. If I failed, well, then I'd be poised for an easy journey back to Wales. I felt the odds were in my favour. All through my expedition General Mendoza had nearly suffocated my adventure with unasked-for help, and when I had been to see him he had told me that if ever I really did need assistance I only had to ask.

I took the bus back to Puerto Natales, where I found I wasn't the only one with problems. Hornero and Jolgorio, in spite of having been carefully looked after and well fed, had become very thin for the first time on the whole expedition.

The vet said it was due to the extreme cold. I knew I must lose no time in getting them back north. The most important promise of all, of course, was the one I had made to them, that I would get them safely back to their stables once their part in the expedition was over. But how was I to do so? My money had almost run out. So had my energy. So, actually, had my air ticket back to England, valid for only one year. But this seemed a small problem compared to the gigantic questions of how to get the horses safely home, and then how to get permission to land on Cape Horn.

Despairingly I looked at the map. When I had been a child in Ireland I had once bought a donkey foal in Kerry and had hitchhiked home in a petrol tanker. The donkey, stuffed into a sack with his ears sticking out, had sat on the seat between me and the long-suffering driver. Hitchhiking north with two fully grown horses might be more difficult.

I had reckoned without the strange magic that surrounded the whole adventure, the way someone had always come to my aid every time it looked as though the expedition was doomed. Now the owner of the ferry *Ro Ro Evangelista* gave me and the horses free passage to Puerto Montt. There, in response to a telephone call, René Varas once again helped us, and using his vast network of contacts arranged for us to get a lift on a series of lorries transporting horses or cattle north. For much of the time the horses had to share trucks with thickly packed cattle.

When we reached Osorno I learnt that René's great horse Quintral had finally died and had had an elaborate funeral. Then it was on to Valdivia, Temuco, Chillán, Longaví and finally to San Fernando – back up my long tattered map. It had taken nearly a year to ride down through Chile. It took only two weeks to travel back. The places we passed through had the same names, and the mountains had similar shapes, but they were not the same.

Eventually we arrived back at the hacienda. I was shocked by the damage it had sustained in the earthquake. The stables

210

too had been shaken to their foundations. The fifteenth-century ivory cross in the chapel had only just been rescued; at least six thousand sixteenth-century crystal glasses had been broken. Scaffolding still stood around the warm red walls of the hacienda itself. Builders would be busy for another six months repairing the damage.

The horses were welcomed as heroes and I as a member of the family. I felt torn apart by conflicting emotions of joy and sorrow as I handed them over. 'I've kept my promise,' I told myself. I felt too emotional to speak and kept having to borrow Germán Claro Lira's green silk handkerchief as I watched Hornero and Jolgorio kick up their heels in the estate's richest field of clover, then bend down to eat, determined to become fat again as soon as possible.

A programme was outlined for them: they would spend the weekdays out at grass, but come into their stables at weekends for extra tonic jabs and to be shown off to visitors to the hacienda. All around their stalls I pasted photos showing them struggling through the sand-drifts and snow-drifts which rule the very different ends of Chile, because just looking at them, thin but otherwise fit, it seemed impossible they had been through so much. The experts and vets had been right, of course. The horses had faced many ordeals where they had had much more courage than knowledge. Indigenous animals bred in the wild region of Aysén would have understood its freezing rivers and bogs, and would have been more used to climbing mountains and to the cold. But would horses other than Hornero and Jolgorio have come all the way with me, would they had adapted to such drastically different conditions in under one year? I didn't know, of course. I never had any other horses. All I knew was that at no time during the journey, even during our most desperate struggles, had I felt like changing them.

The truth was that what I felt for my friends went far beyond ordinary love for an animal, or even ordinary admiration. They, after all, were the ones who had made the

211

expedition. I had simply sat on their backs and had guided, aided and abetted them. Of course I loved them more than any other living thing in South America. Of course I was prejudiced. But all the love in the world would not have got them through if they had not had the quality.

Hornero and Jolgorio were very happy indeed to be back, and quickly forgave the other horses for not believing their stories. I, however, could hardly bear the thought of relinquishing my responsibility for them. They are not your horses, I kept telling myself. They had only been on loan. But if this was true in one sense, in another it was not. They had given me their love, their hearts, their efforts. They had offered me their lives. They belonged to me, more than they belonged to anyone else in the world – except perhaps to themselves. I had great difficulty coping with the fact that soon I would be leaving them, perhaps for ever. Yet I knew I could not really afford to succumb to my feelings. The horses' mission had been accomplished one hundred per cent successfully, but mine had not.

LOG: *23 August 1985; Hacienda Los Lingues*
Goodbye to Hornero and Jolgorio whose courage made it all possible. It is so difficult to say 'thank you' to a horse. Jolgorio, with a twinkle in his eyes and his mouth crammed with lush grass, still tries to nibble the camera – following me so closely it is hard to get a last picture. Hornero, still the proudest horse I have ever met, looks up with big brown eyes as though he is wondering where we are off to next. But I just say '*Ciao*', mount another horse which has brought me out to their field, and gallop away crying. I know I shouldn't, as I have left my horses in what they think is paradise, and 'farewell' is the price I always knew I would have to pay.

*   *   *

212

When I wasn't watching the horses and enjoying the Claro Liras' incomparable hospitality, I was in Santiago, lobbying. My first visit was to General Mendoza. I thought he looked greyer than he had been when I had met him a few months before. He welcome me warmly and soothed me when I spilt the slides I had brought to show him all over the floor of his office. '*No te pongas nerviosa,*' he said. 'Don't be nervous.' I left his office clutching an enormous bronze plaque for 'Valour' and a firm promise that he would personally arrange my visit to Cape Horn with his colleague in the Junta government, Admiral Merino, the head of the Navy.

However, if I had learnt anything by now it was that life is never so simple. Two days later it was in the headlines of all the newspapers: 'MENDOZA RESIGNS!'

On 17 March 1985 three left-wing teachers had been found in a Santiago street with their throats cut. Fourteen carabineros had been accused of the crime and now General Mendoza was being forced to resign to protest his officers' innocence. That night there were cries of 'Assassins!' in the streets and black-and-white water cannon spraying crowds of protesters.

Cape Horn seemed further and further away. Chile was in confusion because of the changes in the government and from the after-effects of the earthquake. Against this background my need to get to Cape Horn did not seem very important even to the kind-hearted Chileans, and I did not blame them. I trailed round a succession of offices in Santiago and everyone said 'No,' very politely. 'You and your horses have already been to Puerto Williams, haven't you?' said one naval official. 'We have done enough.'

'If they were going to take you to Cape Horn I'm afraid they'd have done so by now,' advised John Hickman. He and Jenny welcomed me at the British Embassy Residence whenever I stayed overnight in Santiago. Had it not been for their support and that of the Claro Liras I think I would have given up. As it is, I suspect that even these friends thought I

213

was slightly mad. 'Cape Horn is something you sail around, isn't it?' said John Hickman one day. 'Why on earth do you want to *land* on it?'

I determined to make one last effort. I would go and see the head of the Navy, Admiral Merino, in person. I went back to General Mendoza, now living in seclusion, and persuaded him to write the Admiral on my behalf. Lucía Pinochet, daughter of the President, also wrote, as did Margarita Ducci. She also contacted the Air Force representative on the Junta, General Mattai, on my behalf.

On Monday 19 August, Mónica Krassa, Margarita Ducci's assistant, told me the news. 'The Air Force will take you to Antarctica.'

I was at once excited and disappointed. I would see Antarctica in winter, when even the penguins don't get there, travelling further south than I had ever dreamed, but I still wasn't going to Cape Horn. The Hercules from Punta Arenas to the Chilean Air Force base of Teniente Marsh on King George Island in Antarctica would fly over Cape Horn on the way. At least I would *see* it. Maybe that would have to do. Surely, I told myself, I shouldn't be thinking of Antarctica as merely 'second best'. And perhaps Cape Horn would be a disappointment? Maybe one should not see a legend too close. After all, I tried to comfort myself, it would be terrible to land on Cape Horn, symbol of so much yachting history – and to find that it was just another scruffy little island at the bottom of the world.

The day before I was due to leave for Punta Arenas on the first leg of my Antarctic journey, I was summoned to the Ministry of Defence. 'I hear you have a problem?' said Admiral Gustavo Pheifer. 'Oh no,' I replied, 'but I do have a need.'

I explained to him how very kind the *Armada* had already been to me. But how I did actually *need* to go to Cape Horn. I did not want them to go to any extra trouble on my behalf, or to spend one extra peso. All I wanted was permission to travel on board one of the ships visiting Cape Horn with supplies for the lighthousemen.

The Admiral listened to me kindly and patiently. 'Admiral Merino will personally make the decision tomorrow,' he told me. When he said goodbye there was a twinkle in his eyes – and I felt hopeful.

Chapter Twenty

———————⤳⤲———————

Gasping in the fierce cold, I clung on – a pillion passenger on a small snow buggy. All around me was a fantastic world of white. It was impossible to tell where the carpet of ice and snow ended and the sky began.

This was the winter ice desert of Antarctica. The normal climate, I was told, includes constant blizzards, winds up to eighty miles an hour and temperatures of thirty degrees below zero. The visibility could not have been more than 400 metres.

The penguins and sealions Antarctica is so well known for had been driven away by the harsh weather and would not be back till most visitors arrived to photograph them, next spring. Even the famous sign pointing to London and lots of other cities all over the world was heavily veiled in fast falling snow, its post buried in drifts more than fifteen feet deep.

With great difficulty, because of the slewing and bouncing of the buggy, I got out my camera. Then discovered that there was very little to photograph anyway, except miles and miles of whiteness. This was probably just as well. I had been warned that the extreme cold might crack the lens if I left it uncovered too long.

Yet somehow in spite of all this, the chance to see this extraordinary part of the world when few other visitors do, albeit for a very short time, seemed a great privilege. Antarctica lay all around me. Its beautiful icebergs were hidden behind falling snow, but its heart lay raw and open. No accessories. No distractions. Just wild white splendour.

I owed it all to one of the most extraordinary 'Day Return' trips ever arranged – all the way from Punta Arenas out to Antarctica and back in twenty-four hours. It was organized for me by a kindly Air Force general, who had arranged for me to travel on a Hercules aircraft flying out to Teniente Marsh Airbase on King George Island at latitude 62 degrees south; sharing valuable space with Air Force personnel and their families.

My snow-buggy ride came to an end near the little settlement of Villa Las Estrellas, or 'The Town of the Stars', where the hardy Chilean Air Force community, one of the first to bring women and children with them to Antarctica, lived all year round.

I stretched my senses to try and learn as much as I could during the few hours I had in this amazing continent, and quickly discovered that, in spite of the weather, King George Island was very far from being just a snowy wilderness. I was shown a large red container, as off a ship, which turned out to be the southernmost bank in the world. A similar container housed the post office, selling its own special Antarctic stamps. A much larger red building was the Meteorological Station where I met Augusto Llaxo Eck, the head meteorologist, famous throughout Chile for his work at the South Pole. He welcomed me and patiently explained the complicated patterns of some of the local weather systems. Not far off were the neat little houses of the Air Force families. In spite of the harsh climate, they seemed to lead quite comfortable and very well organized lives. From the inside the homes were run in the same way as, and looked similar to, tidy air force or army houses anywhere in the world, with china ornaments, family photographs, and souvenirs of previous assignments on the mantelpieces. Almost every need is flown in, I was told, 'except perhaps a hairdresser. That is not really hardship, is it?'

The Air Force families all welcomed me with tremendous

217

friendliness, escorting me from house to house for an endless series of cups of tea, and proudly introducing me to little Guisela, just eight months old and the first baby girl actually born in Antarctica.

One of the surprises of my short visit was to learn that more than twenty-five nations are represented in Antarctica, at least six on King George Island itself. 'Every evening,' one woman said, 'we ask ourselves, "Shall we have supper in China tonight? Or shall we eat in Poland? Or is it perhaps time for a Russian dinner with a little vodka?" ' All these countries had bases on the island, each only a few hundred yards apart.

Soon it was time to leave. We waited for a while in the base's small hostelry near the airstrip for a heavy series of snow showers to ease off. Then at last, just before dusk, but still quite early in the afternoon, the Hercules – which was equipped with skis as well as wheels – set off down a trail of icy snowdrifts somewhere beneath which was the airstrip.

As I looked down at the lights of the base I remembered the words of Lisa Marchelli, the wife of one of the helicopter pilots there:

'On a clear night in spring,' she told me, 'you can almost touch the stars here, which is why our community is called Villa Las Estrellas. Then when the sunrise comes, you wait in suspense to see what it will reveal. The beautiful shapes and colours of the great icebergs change every day. Sometimes the whole view will alter completely overnight because an iceberg has drifted away, never to be seen again, or a new one has arrived. In spring come the seals, the sealions, multitudes of birds and thousands of penguins, seemingly similar to each other, but so distinctive in character that pairs who mate remain faithful to each other for life.'

Her words wove a spell. I would keep Antarctica in my heart to come back to one day. Meanwhile Cape Horn lay somewhere in the shadows and clouds below us. My stomach clenched. What had the Admiral decided?

A message was waiting for me as the Hercules landed in Punta Arenas. I was to call on Admiral Fernando Camús, Chief of Naval Zone III, at the headquarters in Punta Arenas. He had Admiral Merino's decision for me.

Heart thumping, I made my way to his elegant office, the other side of the plaza. He smiled. I smiled. He wasn't wearing the sort of expression he'd use for telling bad news. There had been a misunderstanding before, he explained. Now I had been given authority to go on a very special mission. AGS *Yelcho*, built for Southern Ocean winter seas, was bound for Cape Horn where she could land me while delivering supplies to the lighthousemen. Afterwards she would be sailing thirty-five miles south of Cape Horn, across Drake's Passage, to the Diego Ramírez Islands, to collect some engineers who had just finished constructing the islands' first lighthouse. The ship would pick me up in Puerto Williams and he had arranged for me to be flown there early next morning.

I could hardly take it all in. It was like too much wine all at once. I left his office almost bursting with excitement and gratitude. Every hoofprint on the map of Chile was worth it, all the struggles and disappointments.

Back in Puerto Williams, waiting for the *Yelcho* to dock, I was teased by the sailors' wives: 'You can't keep away from this place!' I had now been there three times. The snow had now disappeared from all but the highest mountains and the whole island seemed warmer and greener. A bleating in the bushes near the airstrip betrayed the first new-born lamb of early spring. But the real changes were in my mind. Once I had thought of Puerto Williams as the southernmost town in the world, where but for gravity I might fall off the end of the world into space. Now, after my visit to Antarctica, I considered it quite far north. The glaciers along the Beagle Channel and the condors and the great mountains of Tierra del Fuego opposite no longer amazed me; they were familiar friends, lovely to see again.

219

The curator of the island's museum gave the coming voyage an extra dimension by handing me a huge bundle of forms to fill in. He asked if I would undertake an albatross and penguin survey at Cape Horn and Diego Ramírez; so few civilians manage to get there in winter that the birds' habits at that time of year are little known. He provided me with descriptions of at least five different sorts of albatross to look out for, and many sorts of penguins, carefully schooling me on how to recognize each bird. I didn't know how much I could discover for the curator, but I certainly learnt a lot *from* him.

On 2 September, having been delayed by bad weather, the *Yelcho* at last tied up at the sturdy naval wharf. Comandante Eduardo García Domínguez, his officers and crew – as well as the three ship's dogs – all gave me a warm welcome. The Navigational Officer, Rodrigo Lledo, very chivalrously gave me his own cabin, which lay snug in the heart of the ship, for the voyage.

The glaciers along the Beagle Channel were tinted with gold from an especially glorious sunrise as the ship cast off her warps early next morning. 'ETA Cabo de Hornos will be around 1600 hours this afternoon,' remarked Rodrigo Lledo as we set sail eastward past Isla Gable. I bent back over the navigational chart where he had been showing me the course, so that he couldn't quite see the extent of my excitement. What a beautiful day to return to Cape Horn. Even the *Yelcho*'s name seemed appropriate: in the ancient Mapuche language, it meant 'Spring of Hope'.

The first ship of that name had rescued many survivors from HMS *Endurance* in 1916 during Ernest Shackleton's Antarctic expedition. The present *Yelcho*, built in America in 1942, was an elegant and sturdy grey salvage vessel, with four engines producing 3000 horsepower. She too had built up quite a reputation as a rescue ship, saving many vessels including the Norwegian ship the *Linbald Explorer* when she had been in trouble off King George Island. *Yelcho* had made no less than nineteen journeys to Antarctica since 1962, and had engaged in a great deal of hydrographical and scientific work.

By midday, south of Lennox, the clear golden sky of early morning had given way to high piles of blackest cloud, followed by squalls of hail or sleet. The sea was becoming rougher.

At lunchtime in the Commander's wardroom, all the plates and glasses leapt off the table. I was glad that on this voyage I was not in charge of the cooking – or indeed of the navigation!

Two hours later the Wollaston Archipelago came into view on our starboard side. The ceiling of the sky lifted briefly and the sun gleamed through, revealing the islands as a mysterious maze of green shapes and shadows. Wheeling above the ship were several of what seemed to be the Black Browed Albatross, with a white body, black-tipped wings and bright yellow legs. I thought I could identify them from the smudgy marks above their eyes, but my task was made more difficult by the many large brown seabirds pretending to be albatrosses!

By 1500 hours I could see Isla Deceit and Isla Herschel. The southern end of the aptly named Deceit seemed to consist of a number of great rock teeth sticking straight up from the sea. As though belonging to some giant madman of the Southern Ocean, they foamed as the waves crashed over them. The *Yelcho* was going to have to round them to get to Horn Island. But as we drew closer, the rocks gave the illusion of getting further away, as the wind built up again and another severe hailstorm slashed visibility.

Then all at once, with Deceit abeam, the sky brightened again. For the next twenty minutes we went through a meteorological cocktail of hailstorms and squalls, interspersed with breathless moments of sunshine and crystal-clear visibility. It was as though the Southern Ocean was showing off all the types of weather she had to offer.

Suddenly I saw it. For the first time for thirteen long years

221

I was looking at the unique profile of Cape Horn itself.

It was more magnificent than I remembered. Dark bundles of low cloud clustered over Drake's Passage, but to landward, behind the Hermite group, the sky had patches of pink. Shafts of sunshine piercing the clouds lent extra drama and splendour to the legendary outline of the great rock. As the wind screamed and my mind was flooded with memories, I was almost choked by the incredible wild beauty of the place.

The *Yelcho* anchored in the lee of the island, on its more sheltered east side, near to the only place where it is possible to land men and supplies. Even so, the wind was still gusting 35 to 40 knots as the Zodiac tender came ashore on the little rock beach. It was all the more tricky because the thick bed of kelp close to the shore kept fouling the outboard motor propeller, making it stall. As I began my climb up the steep slope from the beach, I watched the sailors begin to unload four months' supply of food for the three lighthousemen, as well as four months' firewood – and also the heavy new stove which had been ordered for the lighthousemen's hut. Somehow they had to nurse the half-waterlogged dinghy back and forth amid the constant squalls, and then when they had got the whole lot to the beach they still had to drag the cargo up 200 feet.

Catching my breath near the top of the hill, I stooped down and picked some tufty grass as a keepsake. I also found two small stones to take back. The wind roared in my ears.

With one of the *Yelcho's* officers I made my way along a boggy path to a small rickety-looking hut with a sign outside saying, 'Welcome – Cabo de Hornos'. Inside, the lighthousemen had the kettle boiling. They pulled a chair over to the crude wood stove and bade me welcome.

Coffee on Cape Horn with the lighthousemen has to be the ultimate fantasy of any yachtswoman run away to land. As we sipped the scalding liquid, and nibbled the little cakes which they had baked in a tin on their fire, they told me about the hardship of their life at the end of the world. It was very dangerous tending the light in stormy weather and many lighthousemen had lost their lives over the years. The lighthouse itself was on the other side of the island. At best their job was very lonely. The *Yelcho* had brought the first mail they had had for months. When I did my duty and asked about the birds they told me that the penguin colony had left during the harsh winter and hadn't returned yet. However, they proudly introduced me to their puppy Línea, who, they claimed, ought to be in some survey as she was the first dog ever to be born on Horn Island.

Thanking them for the coffee, I left them to re-read their post and sort out their new supplies. I walked southward as far as I could, bracing myself against the wind which I felt might pick me up and fling me out to Drake's Passage, the way it had many before me.

Looking out to sea I could almost see the catamaran *Anneliese*, and hear my children's laughter as they played with long strings of bulbous seaweed. As adventures past and present met, I tried to thank ''im up there'.

I had taken 409 days to get back to Cape Horn. It had been the hardest expedition I had ever done, as well as the most rewarding. Many times the horses and I had almost failed. Many other times the true purpose of my journey had been overshadowed by difficulties, and only some obstinate instinct had kept me going. It had been worth all the tremendous struggle.

Before I left Cape Horn I wrote Hornero's and Jolgorio's names in the lighthousemen's Visitor's Book, the first horses ever to be entered there. It was the end of an odyssey.